PR
6039

After You With
The Milk

A Comedy

Ben Travers

Samuel French—London
New York—Sydney—Toronto—Hollywood

UNIVERSITY OF WINNIPEG
LIBRARY
515 Portage Avenue
Winnipeg, Manitoba R3B 2E9

DISCARDED

© 1985 by Andrew Morgan, as executor of the Estate of the late Ben Travers

1. *This play is fully protected under the Copyright Laws of the British Commonwealth of Nations, the United States of America and all countries of the Berne and Universal Copyright Conventions.*

2. *All rights, including Stage, Motion Picture, Radio, Television, Public Reading, and Translation into Foreign Languages, are strictly reserved.*

3. **No part of this publication may lawfully be reproduced in ANY form or by any means, photocopying, typescript, recording (including video-recording), manuscript, electronic, mechanical, or otherwise—or be transmitted or stored in a retrieval system, without prior permission.**

4. Rights of Performance by Amateurs are controlled by SAMUEL FRENCH LTD, 52 FITZROY STREET, LONDON W1P 6JR, and they, or their author-ized agents, issue licences to amateurs on payment of a fee. It is an infringement of the Copyright to give any performance or public read-ing of the play before the fee has been paid and the licence issued.

5. Licences are issued subject to the understanding that it shall be made clear in all advertising matter that the audience will witness an amateur performance; that the names of the authors of the plays shall be in-cluded on all announcements and on all programmes: and that the integrity of the author's work will be preserved.

The Royalty Fee indicated below is subject to contract and subject to variation at the sole discretion of Samuel French Ltd.

Basic fee for each and every
performance by amateurs   Code M
in the British Isles

In Theatres or Halls seating Six Hundred or more the fee will be subject to negotiation.

In Territories Overseas the fee quoted above may not apply. A fee will be quoted on application to our local authorized agent, or if there is no such agent, on application to Samuel French Ltd, London.

6. The Professional Rights in this play are controlled by Fraser and Dun-lop (Scripts) Ltd, 91 Regent Street, London W1.

The publication of this play does not imply that it is necessarily available for performance by amateurs or professionals, either in the British Isles or Overseas. Amateurs and professionals considering a production are strongly advised in their own interests to apply to the appropriate agents for consent before starting rehearsals or booking a theatre or hall.

ISBN 0 573 01610 0

Printed in Great Britain by Butler & Tanner Ltd, Frome and London

CHARACTERS

Dottie
Ricky
Don
Leila
Fred

The action of the play takes place in the living-room of Fred's house

ACT I

Time—the summer of 1935

ACT I*

Scene 1

The living-room of Fred's house. The heat-wave summer of 1935. Four o'clock in the afternoon

The house is set in by a by-street of the residential area of Kensington. C upstage is the hall with the front door on the R. In the hall is the lower part of the staircase. A broad archway separates the hall from the room itself and there is a passage between the foot of the staircase and off L. The archway is of sufficient width to give a clear view of the hall from the living-room. There may be long curtains at either end of the archway but these are not drawn during the play

In the living-room itself there is a door in the L wall. There are windows in the R wall with gauze curtains and summer side-curtains. There is also a small window in the R back wall, giving a view of the front door outside from the room

The room is furnished elegantly with no expense spared but there is nothing ultra-modern about the furnishings or decorations. The sofa and chair covers are all of light summer material

When the CURTAIN rises, Dottie, wearing a thin summer dress, is lying on the sofa reading. She is feeling the heat and her dress may be disarrayed to keep her as cool as possible. She has taken off her shoes and they are on the floor by the sofa. There is a tumbler with a small amount of whisky and water left in it on the little table beside the sofa

The front door-bell rings

Dottie (*looking up and speaking to herself*) Who's that?

Dottie sighs, sits up and puts her book down. She puts on one shoe, pauses and finishes her drink, then puts on her other shoe

The front-door bell rings loudly

(*Plaintively*) Who is it? (*She rises and fixes her dress*)

Dottie exits into the hall and opens the front door cautiously, just wide enough for her to peer through

Ricky (*off*) Good afternoon. Is this Mr and Mrs Dunn's house?
Dottie Yes. I'm Mrs Dunn. Why?
Ricky (*off*) *You* are? Good Lord.
Dottie Who are you? What do you want?

---

*NB Paragraph 3 on page ii of this Acting Edition regarding photo-copying and video-recording should be carefully read.

Ricky (*off*) No, I only said "Good Lord" like that because you look so young.

Dottie closes the front door

(*Off*) Oh, please open the door.
Dottie No, thank you. You may be one of those men.
Ricky (*off*) I'm not. Please listen. My name's Dunn too. I'm your husband's son.
Dottie No, you're not. He's in Australia.
Ricky (*off*) I know. But I'm here now. I've just got here.
Dottie (*in two minds*) Really? Truly? (*She opens the door again a little*) One minute—what's your name?
Ricky (*off*) I've told you. Dunn.
Dottie Don't be silly—your Christian name?
Ricky (*off*) Ricky. Rickaby. Rickaby Dunn.
Dottie Good heavens. (*She opens the door wider*)

Ricky enters. He is dressed in a new summer suit and new shoes

Dottie is doubtful and distrusting

I oughtn't to let you in. Your father wouldn't have.
Ricky Oh, then he's still alive?
Dottie Of course he is. He's in hospital.
Ricky Still there?
Dottie No, again. But he's not bad this time. He'll be out in a day or two.
Ricky Oh. Well, I must wait and see him then.
Dottie If he'll see you. And you can't wait here. You can come in for a minute or two because it's so hot ...

Dottie enters the living-room. Ricky follows Dottie downstage

Ricky Yes, isn't it?
Dottie And then you must go away again.
Ricky You mean—right bang off?
Dottie Yes. I've heard about you, you see.
Ricky I guess you have. But I'm really quite harmless.
Dottie That's what they always say.
Ricky Who do?
Dottie The men.
Ricky These men—I'm sorry I don't quite—what men?
Dottie They break in and rape women and things. Especially in this very hot weather. It makes them want.
Ricky I don't rape. I don't see there's any fun in it. Do you?
Dottie I don't know; I've never had it done to. And if you don't rape you do other awful things and always have.
Ricky I know my father says so.
Dottie Yes. So why aren't you still in Australia?
Ricky I felt I ought to see the old man again. I heard he'd had a stroke.
Dottie That was months ago.

Ricky Yes, but I'd only just heard. I met a woman in Sydney who'd been in Kenya when you were there and knew all about you. Rosie Roberts.

Dottie Rosie—Oh, yes. She eloped to Australia with an Indian photographer.

Ricky She told me the whole thing—how the old man had sold up his estate in Kenya and come to live in London and had married you and had a stroke.

Dottie It wasn't marrying me gave him the stroke. Did Rosie say that?

Ricky No, no. Sorry. You married him five or six years ago, didn't you?

Dottie Yes. In Nairobi. He had no strokes then. Quite the opposite. I'm afraid he may get another now with you turning up like this.

Ricky Oh dear. I felt it was my duty. I got on the first ship I could. I only landed today. I worked my passage all the way home.

Dottie In this heat? Oh, then you'd better sit down for a minute.

Ricky Thank you. (*He sits*) I'm glad I called in anyhow.

Dottie Why?

Ricky To have discovered you. You're so much younger than I expected. And, if I may say so, much more attractive.

Dottie (*instinctively pleased*) Am I? (*Reacting*) Oh, it's no good your saying things like that. And did you imagine that your father had married some old hideosity?

Ricky Well ... but fancy your consenting to marry *him*.

Dottie If you're going to say rude things about him ...

Ricky No, I'm not. I came on purpose to try not to.

Dottie You've always hated each other. Why? He's a dear old man really. I'm very fond of him.

Ricky Then he must have improved with age. No, no—I didn't mean that either. But you know what he's like—no, no, you don't. You love him of course. Anyhow, you married him.

Dottie And I'm very glad I did.

Ricky Good. But ...

Dottie But what?

Ricky You're such miles younger than he is.

Dottie Heavens, yes. Why shouldn't I be?

Ricky Honestly, I would like to make it up with him. Now that he's so near his grave.

Dottie Don't say that; he's not. Besides, he wants to be cremated.

Pause

(*In a tone of finality*) Well ...

Ricky (*rising unwillingly*) Oh dear—has it come to that already?

Dottie (*after a moment's thought*) No. Sit down again. I'm not being like myself. I don't want you to think I'm—unfriendly.

Ricky I don't. And I wonder if I'm as bad as you've been given to think.

Dottie You don't look it but you must be—for Fred to be like he is about you.

Ricky He was like that from the moment I was born. He didn't think I was really his son. He told my mother so directly he saw me.

Dottie He was always argumentative.

Ricky My mother buzzed off somewhere and soon died. And there he was, left with me.

Dottie Does he still think you're not his. He never told me you weren't.

Ricky (*shrugging*) I think he decided to make the best of a bad job.

Dottie Whether it was his or someone else's.

Ricky Anyhow, we could never get on. It got worse and worse. Finally I quit and went to Australia.

Dottie (*gently*) I wonder whether he'd be different about you now.

Ricky He might. These strokes may have made him a bit feeble-minded.

Dottie He's not nearly as feeble-minded as I am. If it were him and not me you wouldn't still be here. (*She moves to the drinks table*) Soda or plain or just ice?

Ricky You're very kind. Just a little phtt from the syphon.

Dottie prepares two drinks while they continue talking

After all, why should he change. He's always been the same with me ever since he beat hell out of me as a kid.

Dottie That was silly of him. It can only have made you worse.

Ricky It did. When I was sent to school here in England it wasn't the old story that I got into bad company. I was the bad company the other boys got into.

Dottie Then at least your schooldays were happy.

Ricky While they lasted. When I was seventeen I was expelled from Charterhouse.

Dottie What had you done?

Ricky One of the housemaids.

Dottie It was nice that you were normal anyhow. (*She hands Ricky his drink*)

Ricky Thank you so much.

Dottie It must be so difficult at public schools when you've only each other—all boys together. Like those poor gaolbirds. I'm always so sorry for them about that. Never mind them now—go on about yourself. So then you went back to Kenya ...

Ricky Yes, in disgrace. I worked on the estate, always at daggers drawn with the old man.

Dottie (*gently*) Was that all his fault?

Ricky No, a lot mine. Eventually he got me a job with a chap who sold tractors.

Dottie (*with sudden amused interest*) Oh, I know about that. It was Don Raeburn. And one afternoon you were caught in bed with his wife, Mabel.

Ricky My father told you, did he?

Dottie No. Don Raeburn told me himself. He lives in London now—quite close to here.

Ricky looks startled and becomes quite agitated

Ricky Good Lord, does he?

Dottie He's in some City thing—import and export or both or something.

Ricky Is he still friendly with my father?

Dottie Yes, he's (*hesitating*)—often in here. Why?

Ricky He'd go out of his way to dish any hopes I've got.

Dottie Yes, he's always been annoyed about you and Mabel.

Ricky Annoyed? Talk about my father hating me—I say, don't let Don know I'm back in England—please don't.

Dottie All right, I won't. Of course not. But Don's not here now; he's up north somewhere.

Ricky Oh, good. He can't be too far away for me.

Dottie He's got another wife now. A very nice girl. I've made great friends with her. Fred says she's a great improvement on Mabel.

Ricky He didn't know Mabel as well as I did.

Dottie Was it on account of Mabel you went to Australia?

Ricky Well, I couldn't stay in Kenya with Don around. There'd have been murder. And I thought if I quit he might take Mabel back.

Dottie (*keenly*) Then you did really go out of kindness to Mabel?

Ricky Sort of. I should have known Don better.

Dottie And in Australia—did you carry on the same way there?

Ricky I did all the things one does in Australia with sheep and docks and mines and beer. I did quite well at times but it never lasted.

Dottie I meant—about women?

Ricky On and off. Nothing that anyone has any regrets about.

Dottie How good and sensible. And you can't have done badly in other ways. You look quite prosperous.

Ricky I landed with twenty-eight quid. I went to Harrods and got fitted out. I thought I'd better look fairly civilized.

Dottie That's very nice and clean of you but you must have spent all your money.

Ricky Isn't it hell nowadays?

Dottie What about your luggage?

Ricky Only one old suitcase. I parked it at Harrods.

Dottie Aren't you going to get it out again before they close?

Ricky No hurry. I like being here. That is if you don't mind.

Dottie No, I don't now. (*After a pause*) I'm surprised at you.

Ricky Why, what have I done now?

Dottie Coming over like this and going and spending all your money like that. Are you really hoping to get reconciled?

Ricky (*with a blunt laugh*) It's a long shot but I've always gambled a bit.

Dottie Don't think me horrid but—it's really the thought of Fred's money, isn't it?

Ricky Yes.

Dottie (*pleased*) That's honest of you.

Ricky I guess it's best to be honest with *you*.

Dottie Yes, it is. And I'd like you to get some of it if you can. There's masses of it. There was even before he sold the estate. I'm glad there was. Oh, the money wasn't why I married him, at least, not my first reason. But I've become much fonder of him since I got it.

Ricky What was the first reason?

Dottie I went to stay with friends in Nairobi. I met him there. He really loved me right away and I—sort of—pitied him; he seemed lonely and uncared-for. I felt drawn towards him. He was so pleading and pathetic.

Ricky (*incredulously*) My father? Pathetic?

Dottie Well, pleading anyhow. And of course he offered me all I wanted. That came second but I thought oh well, if God chose to put it in my way . . .

Ricky It may not have been God. It may have been the devil.

Dottie Yes, it's often difficult to know which is which. But it's turned out beautifully. I look after him and he looks after me. I'm in what they used to call a bed of roses.

Ricky Delightful. So long as it's all right about who else is in the bed.

Dottie I suppose I really married him out of kindness. But I'm like that. I always want to be kind to everybody. Like you—I'd like to try and help you with Fred. But why *does* he hate you so? You must have been wicked to him.

Ricky No—well, perhaps sometimes a bit wicked back. And, please, I'm not asking you to help me. That might upset him. I'll tackle him on my own. I suppose I'd better not go and see him in hospital?

Dottie Oh, no. You might have to stay in hospital yourself. I'll break it to him gently that you're here.

Ricky (*gratefully*) Will you?

Dottie Of course. I tell you I enjoy helping people even if they don't deserve it. I'm not a do-gooder, though I don't see there's any harm in being one. I don't give much money to charities and things. I do kind things which turn out to be frightfully mistaken and troublesome. I'm impulsive too. I do and say things on the spur of the moment. And drop bricks. People laugh at me about it.

Ricky I bet they love you all the same.

Dottie Oh yes, they do. (*She takes Ricky's glass and mixes him another drink*)

Ricky I don't see how they couldn't. I'm glad I came here if it were only to meet you.

Dottie Thank you. I'm glad you feel that I'm encouraging.

Ricky I do. You must have improved my father a lot.

Dottie I don't know. He dotes on *me* but I don't think he's changed much otherwise. He's still rather flarey at times. And he still loves to argue. But not with me for long because I always give way.

Ricky That was my trouble with him. Neither of us ever gave way.

Dottie How frightfully stupid. (*She hands Ricky his drink*)

Ricky Thank you so much.

Dottie I oughtn't to be giving you another drink. You should be going to get that suitcase.

Ricky My word, the old man's luckier than he deserves . . .

Dottie So am I. Our marriage is just what marriage ought to be.

Ricky Oh? And what's that?

Dottie I think marriage is—have you ever been married?

Ricky shakes his head

I think marriage is something separate—apart from anything else in life; something that's sort of solid and settled and that's always there and always will be. So many people don't look on it that way. They just get together and marry and after a bit they squabble and part and only because they both want a little occasional—well, change of air.

Ricky Yes. But I suppose it depends a bit on where they go to get the change of air. (*After a pause, rather cheekily*) Do *you*—travel much?

Dottie looks at Ricky shrewdly. Her tone changes and she becomes practical though still friendly

Dottie Drink that up; you must go and get that suitcase. What do you do then? Have you got anywhere to stay?

Ricky That's all right; I'll find some small hotel or somewhere.

Dottie Hotel? You can't afford that. You've no idea what they charge nowadays, even the little fleabags. You can come back here; I've a perfectly good spare bedroom.

Ricky My God, talk about your being kind . . .

Dottie We've had all that. I'm so glad I can be.

Ricky Not so glad as I am. It's wonderful of you.

Dottie No, it isn't. I wouldn't want you to go anywhere else.

Ricky You wouldn't?

Dottie No. I never imagined you'd be—like you are.

Ricky I never imagined anybody would be like *you* are.

Dottie Well, that's all to the good, isn't it? I'll go and get your room ready. Fred might not like your being here, but . . .

Ricky Not like it? He'd be rabid.

Dottie Yes, and I don't do anything that'll worry him, poor old dear. So I won't tell him.

Ricky And surely it's quite reasonable. After all, you are my step-mother.

Dottie Oh, so I am. I hadn't really thought of that.

Ricky (*laughing*) You're a step in the right direction if ever there was one. What's your name by the way?

Dottie Dottie. Dorothy really. But I'm always Dottie. And just about right for me.

Ricky I'm Rickaby but always Ricky.

Dottie Yes, I know. Go on now, you'll have to hurry and it's so hot. Have you enough money for taxis?

Ricky Yes, I'm okay. (*He kisses Dottie on the cheek*) Thank you, dear Dottie. (*He kisses Dottie on the other cheek*) Thank you, reverend step-mother.

Ricky exits through the front door

Dottie stands wide-eyed. She looks at the front door and away again

Dottie Gosh.

CURTAIN

Scene 2

The same. One hour later

Dottie is sitting on the sofa with her shoes on and not reading. There is a long drink on the table beside her. Her attitude is expectant

The front-door bell rings. Dottie goes quickly to answer the door

On opening the front door Dottie is shocked and steps back exclaiming

Dottie Don ...
   Don enters. He is dressed in a business man's suit. He puts his arms around Dottie and speaks heartily

Don Hallo, lovie. (*He lowers his voice*) Is he here?
Dottie No, he's still in hospital.

Don releases Dottie and comes downstage into the living-room

Don Aha. I was counting on that.

Dottie closes the front door and moves downstage
Dottie (*as she moves*) But Don, why didn't you tell me you were coming?
Don Didn't know myself till this morning. I only just had time to catch the train.
Dottie But haven't you been home?
Don I looked in. Leila was out, thank God. I left her a note.
Dottie Why, what did you tell her?
Don Oh, simply—I had to go out and dine with a man I met on the train—important business. Huh—I wonder how often that's been said. Well, come on, my love, give us a kiss.

Dottie kisses Don quickly on the cheek

Don No, a real one. What's the matter with you?
Dottie Nothing, dear. At least—(*She kisses him on the mouth abruptly*) More by-and-by.
Don What's all this? Why aren't you like you always are?
Dottie It's all so sudden and unexpected.
Don Makes it all the better. Come on—we're just right. A couple of hours before we go to dinner.

Don moves to kiss Dottie again but she backs away

Dottie No, wait, Don. Do give me time to tell you.
Don Tell me what?
Dottie We can't. Not now. I've got somebody else coming here.
Don (*aggressively*) What? Who?
Dottie Oh—just a friend.
Don Coming when?

Dottie Any time now.
Don How long for?
Dottie For the night. To stay here. In the spare bedroom.
Don Oh, be damned to that. Who is she?
Dottie Well, actually, it's a man.
Don Actually—I always love that actually. My God, Dottie, are you up to something?
Dottie Don't be silly. He's just a relation. A cousin.
Don A friend you said.
Dottie Yes, well actually he's a sort of distant cousin.
Don Oh, actually is he? He needn't think he's coming here.
Dottie He is, I tell you. He turned up here this evening, hoping to see Fred.
Don What about?
Dottie I think he wants to raise some money.
Don Well, give him some money and tell him to bugger off. Letting him in here—you're too kind-hearted, that's your trouble.
Dottie I like to be. It's a pity more people aren't.
Don Come on; I'll go to your room. And you get rid of him and come on up.
Dottie I can't send him away. You get so impatient, Don.
Don Yes, I damn well am impatient. I've been waiting for this—thinking of it all the way on the train.
Dottie Well, you must bottle it up, dear. Now, sit down and I'll give you a little drink.
Don Little one? (*Indicating her drink*) *You* look as if you're lashing into it all right. (*He sits*)

Dottie gives Don her drink

Dottie I don't want it now. You have it. There. (*She moves behind Don and strokes his head*)
Don (*grumpily*) I don't much care for this sweetie-pie stuff either.

Don drinks

Dottie Yes, you do; you know you do.
Don (*relenting*) Yes, yes; all right.

Don turns his face up, kisses Dottie and blows his cheeks out

But, my God, this heat. There's never been anything like it. I can't wait to get my clothes off.
Dottie Then take them off—upstairs I mean. You can have a shower and wait there in my room.
Don That's better—that's what I said all along. (*He finishes his drink and rises*) And tell this distant cousin he can get a damn sight more distant.
Dottie It's all rather difficult.
Don Why, what d'you mean?
Dottie It's the sort of muddle I seem to get into.

The front-door bell rings

There he is now.

Don Good. The sooner he's here the sooner he quits.

Don exits upstairs

Dottie goes into the hall, makes certain Don is out of sight, then opens the front door

Ricky enters carrying a well-worn suitcase

Dottie puts her fingers to her lips, gestures to Ricky to put down the suitcase and follow her. She looks upstairs quickly

Dottie enters the living-room and Ricky follows

Ricky (*in a hushed tone*) What's the matter? Someone upstairs?

Dottie Yes. It's all right. He can't hear from there.

Ricky Good Lord; not the old man?

Dottie No. Worse.

Ricky (*puzzled*) Worse?

Dottie Don Raeburn.

Ricky (*startled*) Don? You said he was in the north.

Dottie So he was. But he's come back suddenly. Like you did too.

Ricky But why is he here? And upstairs?

Dottie He's having a shower.

Ricky Why?

Dottie Well—it's terribly hot weather.

Ricky But why here?

Dottie He did go home but his wife's out.

Ricky Can't he shower in his own house without his wife?

Dottie Perhaps he likes to have her looking on.

Ricky (*as if to say "oh, rubbish" pleasantly*) Oh, Dottie.

Pause

Dottie looks perplexed, then gives in

Dottie Oh, what's the use? You've got to know, that's all. I'm afraid you may get a shock.

Ricky I've had a pretty good one already.

Dottie When Fred's not here Don sometimes comes to see me. And not only to *see* me. You know what I mean.

Ricky (*incredulously*) Don Raeburn—and you?

Dottie It began when Fred was in hospital that long first time. Don had always been like that about me.

Ricky And you let him? Him?

Dottie He's not happy at home like I am. He's got a very nice pretty young wife—I told you, didn't I? She and I are very fond of each other. But Don doesn't get on with her.

Ricky (*seriously; bitterly*) She with him you mean.

Dottie I felt I had to try to console him.

Ricky Console him—that's good.

Dottie Yes, but I must be fair, I was rather ready myself. I'd always been keen on it and it had—given me up and I hadn't had it for so long and was so sort of pining. In fact if it hadn't been for Don I think I'd have gone out and tried to get a policeman or someone.

Ricky (*still bitter*) We all get like that at times, but Don Raeburn, my God ...

Dottie Don't be disgusted with me, Ricky. I've always been faithful to Fred, at heart I mean. It was all right when we first married; he was like an old tiger. But he soon sort of dried up. I had to do what I could about it, but only after Fred couldn't.

Ricky Nobody's going to blame you for that but—with him of all people. I'm sorry but I don't think I can stay here now.

Dottie Don't say that, Ricky; don't. If it wasn't Don you wouldn't like whoever it was. Men never like other men who go with women they like. And I had to take pity on Don. Honestly, I think I'd have done it for his sake even if I hadn't wanted it myself. Out of kindness to him.

Ricky (*studying Dottie and softening*) I've never met anyone like you, Dottie.

Dottie (*decisively*) It's a pity more people aren't like me.

Ricky All this being kind to people and going as far as this with it.

Dottie Well, what greater kindness could there be? Especially when it means enjoying yourself at the same time.

Ricky With Don, that's what I can't get over.

Dottie You can't talk. You did it with Mabel.

Ricky Mabel's not you.

Dottie (*softly*) Isn't she? You mean that's really why you're so disappointed? Because it's me?

Ricky Yes. All right then that's what it is. I'm jealous.

Dottie Oh, Rickie; how sweet of you.

Dottie and Ricky study each other

Ricky Is he going to be here long?

Dottie Until dinner-time. Then he'll take me to dinner. And then he'll go home. I hope.

Ricky Waiting for you up there now, is he?

Dottie He's expecting me, you see. I didn't want him this evening ...

Ricky Then tell him so.

Dottie I can't without hurting his feelings.

Ricky Then hurt them. No, that wouldn't be you. So what? Am I to go out again?

Dottie I hate you to have to. You could stay in your room. Only I suppose Don wouldn't like doing it with you along the landing.

Ricky But, good Lord, you haven't told him *I'm* here?

Dottie Of course not. I said you were a distant cousin staying the night.

Ricky So long as we don't meet. You don't want a fight on your hands. (*Resignedly*) Okay—I'll go out again right away.

Dottie But you will come back, won't you?

Ricky Yes, now I will—later on.

Dottie Have a good dinner yourself. I'll give you some money.

Ricky No, I can manage. (*He indicates his suitcase*) I'll take that thing to my room if he's not about.

Dottie No, he's safely in mine. I'll show you yours. Oh, Ricky, thank you for being so understanding about me. It doesn't really matter, you know, because ...

Ricky Because what?

Dottie Because it hasn't anything to do with real love.

Ricky I should hope not. Not in his case.

Dottie It's only what I said this evening about a little change of air. Don't blame me; you said you didn't.

Ricky (*kindly*) You? I wouldn't blame you if it were the hunchback of Notre-Dame.

Dottie Poor hunchback. I should think he might be rather interesting.

Dottie exits upstairs, Ricky following with his suitcase

(*Off*) It's the first room. Bring it in here.

A door closes upstairs. The telephone rings six or more times

Don enters hastily from upstairs. He is wearing a bath-gown and is carrying a small towel. His hair is ruffled

Don looks at the telephone apprehensively, throws the towel in the chair, lifts the receiver gingerly and listens without speaking. He is greatly startled and lays the receiver aside

Dottie enters hurriedly from upstairs

Don moves to meet her speaking quietly but agitatedly

Don Look out; it's Leila.

Dottie Don—you've got on Fred's bath-gown.

Don (*agitatedly*) It's Leila I tell you.

Dottie You shouldn't wear it. It seems to bring Fred into it.

Don points exasperatedly to the telephone

Don Leila.

Dottie Oh dear; is it? (*She picks up the receiver and speaks, ingenuously at first*) Hallo? Who is it? ... Leila. (*Gushingly*) Leila, dear, how are you? ... What, dear? ... Don? Oh, is he back? ... Here? No, why should he be? ... What, dear? I don't quite understand ... (*In a shocked tone*) Leila, what on earth—are you joking or something? ... Leila, you can't really think? ... The telephone—took the receiver off? That was someone who's staying here, a cousin ... Leila, what is all this, I simply ... Cousin's name? What's that got to do with it? ... Oh, very well then, his name's Bertram Rogers ... Now, listen, Leila; you're being most utterly ... (*She replaces the receiver slowly*) She knows.

Don She can't know. She's just guessing.

Dottie We can't go on now. You'd better get dressed and go home.

Don I've told her I'm dining out, haven't I?

Dottie Oh, yes. With the man on the train. What a feeble thing to say.

Don What did she say on the phone?

Dottie The usual sort of thing—"You needn't think I don't know" and all that. She said she knows you're here now.

Don How can she? She hasn't a clue.

Dottie Get dressed anyhow. We'll have an early dinner and then you can go straight home.

Don Damn. It will be safer I suppose. But we'll still have time back here directly after dinner.

Dottie Oh, Don; with indigestion? No, dear.

Don Well, we'll see. What about this confounded Bertram Rogers?

Dottie He's upstairs; waiting to go out too.

Don Well, tell him to skip the waiting too. Blast all this.

Don exits upstairs forgetting his towel

Dottie speaks after he's gone

Dottie Have I time to change? Never mind—I'll go as I am. No, I've just time ...

The telephone rings

Oh ... (*She picks up the receiver*) Leila, is that you again? ... Oh, I beg your pardon; yes, I'm Mrs Dunn ... No, really—oh, that's wonderful ... Yes, I'll come and get him; what time? ... Oh, then I'll be waiting for him here ... yes, ten o'clock onwards. How kind of the doctor. Give him my love, my husband I mean.... Yes; thank you so much.

Ricky enters from upstairs

Ricky He's back in your room; I heard him. Can I have a latchkey?

Dottie There's one in the writing-table drawer. Ricky, I've just heard— Fred's coming back tomorrow morning.

Ricky Oh dear; so soon. Then that'll be it, won't it.

Dottie And it's all right about him. (*She indicates upstairs*) Nothing to-night. His wife's getting nosey so we're going out now. Instead of doing it.

Ricky I'm glad, Dottie, terribly glad. But I bung off first, do I?

Dottie Yes, go now. And you needn't be too late coming back.

Ricky You won't hear me come in. I'll be here already. Look, there are about a dozen keys in this drawer.

Dottie I'll find it for you.

Dottie moves to Ricky by the writing-table and searches for the key

Don enters from upstairs. He is fully dressed and speaks as he enters

Don Dottie, I left a towel here; you'd better ...

Don breaks off as he sees Ricky. He is completely taken aback. Don and Ricky stare at each other in silence. Don speaks in a tone of fierce irony to Dottie

Bertram Rogers is good.

Ricky (*to Dottie*) Who's he?

Dottie You. It was the first name that came into my head.

Ricky I'm not very keen on Bertram.

Ricky decides to play it cool. Don is fierce

Don Rogers is appropriate anyhow. (*To Dottie*) What the hell is he doing here?

Dottie (*indignantly*) Why shouldn't he be here? (*More calmly*) He's come to see Fred and make friends again.

Don Has he, by God. A fat chance he's got—I'll see to that.

Dottie (*sharply*) No, you won't. Don't you dare to interfere.

Don Here. With you.

Ricky And the same to you.

Don Don't you dare utter. (*To Dottie*) And you telling me he was some damned cousin.

Ricky Distant.

Dottie I told you that because you weren't to be trusted.

Ricky As you have just so clearly indicated.

Don Letting him stay here in this house. That'll please Fred, won't it?

Dottie No, it won't. Any more than it would please Fred to know that you're here. And what for.

Don That's right. Give me away. And yourself.

Ricky Don't worry. I'm only amazed at the extent of her benevolence.

Don That'll do. You stop talking high-falutin' cock and get out.

Dottie Now stop it, Don. I won't have rows in this house. It's no good your being insulting to him. You're only here to do to me what he did to Mabel. (*She is now quite complacent*)

Don That was something entirely different.

Dottie Of course it was different. That's the only reason why people do it. Because it's different with everybody.

Ricky Especially with the hunchback of Notre-Dame.

Don What the hell are you talking about?

The door bell rings. They all look surprised. Don moves to look through the window commanding a view of the porch

Oh, my God—Leila.

Dottie Leila?

Ricky Who's Leila?

Dottie The wife. I told you she was nosey. Leave it to me. Don, go in the dining-room. (*She points* L) No, that's too near. Go through the back door and wait outside.

Don Oh, be damned to that.

Dottie (*commandingly*) Go on. Do.

Don Hell, what a mess-up. To say nothing of finding that bastard here.

The door bell rings

Dottie (*to Don*) Go on I tell you. I must let her in.

Don Why?
Dottie To tell her you're not here of course.
Don Well, be careful what you say. You know what you're like.

Don moves to exit L, *remembers his towel and picks it up, then exits* L

Dottie Ricky, dear, you go upstairs.
Ricky Can't I be here, discovered?
Dottie No, I'll see her first and call you down. Be nice to her.
Ricky I'll try.
Dottie And remember you're not yourself. You're Bertram Rogers.
Ricky Bertram—I do dislike that.
Dottie It can't be helped.

There is a prolonged ring of the door bell

   Ricky exits upstairs

   (*Calling*) Coming. (*She ensures Ricky is out of sight then goes to open the front door*)

   Leila enters, wearing a day dress

Leila moves downstage into the living-room. She is very self-confident. Dottie closes the front door and follows Leila

Leila (*talking as she enters*) That took a bit of organizing didn't it?
Dottie Leila, you're really being very silly.
Leila Knowing Don, I think that's what you're being.
Dottie Why have you come here like this?
Leila To have a few words with Don. Where is he? Taking cover some-where.
Dottie I told you. Only my cousin is here.
Leila (*contemptuously*) Cousin. It's a pity I came so soon. I might have caught you and Don hard at it.
Dottie That's silly. As if I'd have stopped to go down and answer the door.
Leila When Fred was in hospital all that time Don was here almost every afternoon.
Dottie (*taken aback*) Who told you that?
Leila I didn't need telling. I observed for myself.
Dottie Leila, how sneaky. But you couldn't have seen anything. You must have been very disappointed.
Leila That's more than you were. I didn't care much at the time—I was having a little flutter of my own ...
Dottie Oh, Leila, were you? Who with?
Leila But now—when he comes here to you straight from King's Cross ...
Dottie He did not, I tell you ...
Leila This is the finish, darling. And I'll damn well stay here and tell him so.
Dottie That's nice for me. I've got things to do.
Leila Then you won't be doing them with Don.
Dottie I've got my cousin to see to.

Leila (*laughing ironically*) Oh, this cousin. Why does the alibi always have to be a cousin? Really, Dottie, you are the most transparent liar.

Dottie (*indignantly*) I am not transparent. All right then, you wait a minute.

Dottie moves to the foot of the stairs and calls

Bertram . . .

Ricky (*off, cheerfully*) Hallo.

Dottie Come down here.

Leila loses her confidence and looks puzzled. She ignores Dottie's confident smile

Ricky enters from upstairs. He assumes a rather exaggerated gaiety

Leila surveys Ricky and immediately likes the look of him. Dottie looks pleased with herself

Dottie Here he is—Mrs Raeburn—my cousin Bertram . . .

Ricky Rogers.

Dottie Rogers.

Ricky (*to Leila*) Hallo.

Leila Hal-lo. I didn't think you really existed.

Ricky I'm glad you do. (*To Dottie*) Her name again?

Leila Leila.

Ricky Yes, what a nice name. Mine, I'm afraid, is Bertram. I'm waiting to catch up with my god-parents.

Leila You can always be Bertie. Bertie's rather sweet. Where on earth did you get him from, Dottie?

Dottie He lives in the country.

Leila (*to Ricky*) Where?

Ricky Oh, in the bush. You know—a long way away.

Dottie He farms.

Leila He doesn't look much like a farmer to me.

Ricky I only do it in a small way—pigs and gumboots and manure. It's very monotonous. Monotonous manure—it sounds like a song, doesn't it? Be—my—monotonous manure . . .

Dottie He pops up sometimes to visit me.

Leila Why haven't I heard of you before? And aren't you rather in the way here tonight?

Ricky Am I? What of?

Dottie Leila's got some mad idea that her husband's here with me tonight.

Leila So he is. He's probably waiting fuming in your bed.

Dottie He is *not* in my bed. Is he?

Ricky I haven't heard any fuming. What about giving Leila a drink?

Dottie She didn't come here for that.

Leila No, I certainly did not. (*To Ricky*) I'll have a gin and it, half and half on the rocks.

Ricky moves to the drinks table

Ricky I'll fix it.

Dottie (*put out*) Oh, Ricky, must you?

Leila Ricky?

Ricky That's her pet name for me.

Leila Ricky? Not short for Rickaby by any chance?

Ricky (*to Dottie*) There's no need for any secret about it now, is there?

Dottie Oh, very well then—he's really Fred's son.

Leila Rickaby Dunn. But this is terrific. You must be the lad who performed on Mabel.

Ricky I am. Or was. One or two lumps of ice?

Leila One. Do tell me, what was Mabel like?

Ricky In appearance? Or bed?

Dottie No, Leila, please. We don't want to go back into Mabel now.

Leila But why all this Bertram stuff?

Dottie We were keeping him dark because Fred doesn't know he's here. Fred doesn't like him, you see.

Leila Doesn't like him—my God, you should hear Don.

Dottie Well, that proves that Don isn't here, doesn't it?

Leila What does? Of course he's here.

Leila takes her drink from Ricky

Thanks.

Dottie (*warming up*) Oh, don't go on—sitting there and being ridiculous and starting to drink. I've a lot to do. Fred's coming home tomorrow morning.

Leila Oh, I'm glad—dear old Fred. (*To Ricky*) Do tell me all about Mabel.

Dottie (*genuinely struck with an idea*) I know—I've an idea. Ricky's just going out, all on his own—

Leila How very accommodating of him.

Dottie Why don't you go out to dinner with him?

Ricky reacts, not liking this proposal at all

Ricky What? No, listen, Dottie ...

Leila That's one way of getting rid of me. Don't be so dumb.

Dottie But you like Ricky—you've taken to him.

Ricky No, she hasn't.

Leila Yes, I have; very much. That's not the point.

Dottie He can tell you all about Mabel and everything.

Ricky No, I wouldn't. (*Pointedly*) It wouldn't be kind to Mabel.

Leila Oh, I'd quite like to dine with Ricky later on, when I've disposed of Don.

Dottie becomes highly indignant

Dottie Leila, stop being like this; it's hateful of you and you know how I hate people hating.

Leila Try hating yourself for a change. It's about time.

Dottie Now you're being angry with me of all people. When I hate anybody to be angry too.

Ricky Now, please—Dottie—girls …
Leila I'm not in the least angry.
Dottie Yes, you are.
Leila I'm not. But really—trying to send me to dinner with Ricky so that you can have dinner with Don. And not only dinner.
Dottie Don't be so damn silly. You know perfectly well that Don's dining with his friend off the train.
Leila Oh so he is. And how did you know that, Dottie.
Dottie (*aghast*) I've done it again.

Pause

Leila finishes her drink and rises

Leila All right then. I *will* go with Ricky.
Ricky No. I'm sorry; but after all this …
Dottie Yes, go with her, Ricky. I want you to.
Ricky No, I can't. I won't.
Dottie It'll help me. Here, come here. You haven't a latchkey. I'll give you mine. (*She picks up her bag*)
Leila (*to Ricky*) I'm going home to change. You can come and wait for me if you like.
Ricky I'll come along later.
Dottie No, now. Here you are—here's my key.

Ricky stands by Dottie. He makes protesting gestures and indicates the whereabouts of Don. Dottie acknowledges silently and hands Ricky the key and a fistful of Treasury notes

Go along, dear Ricky. I know what I'm doing—as much as I ever do.

Leila moves upstage

Leila Well, are you coming or not?
Dottie Yes, he is.

Ricky reluctantly puts the notes in his pocket

Leila (*calling*) You needn't come home, Don. Or try to see me if you do. This is the finish. That's really all I came here to tell you.
Dottie Don't be unkind to him, Leila.

Leila moves to the front door

He won't be staying on here you know.
Leila Well, I don't care. He'd better go to his bloody Club.

Leila exits through the front door

Ricky dallies a moment looking at Dottie. Dottie smiles

Dottie It's all right. He'll be gone long before you come back.

Ricky unwillingly follows Leila out and closes the door behind him

Dottie goes into the hall, faces L and calls loudly

You can come back in now.

Dottie re-enters the living-room

Don enters from L *of the hall and moves downstage*

Did you hear all that?

Don Not a word. I went outside. A bit *infra dig* but I thought it safer.

Dottie You needn't have. Leila knows all about us.

Don She can't.

Dottie She does. I told her.

Don (*incredulous*) Told her?

Dottie I did what you said I might—I dropped a brick.

Don (*more in sadness than anger*) Dottie, you are the most ...

Dottie (*cutting in*) I lied as long as I could. I wish I hadn't now. I hate lying. Especially if I'm caught out.

Don You confessed to her?

Dottie Only by mistake. But I'm glad really. It makes me feel happier about it.

Don Oh, does it, what about me? Did she know I was here?

Dottie Yes, she left some rude messages. But I'm sure she'll forgive us. She said she didn't really care.

Don Huh—I know better. What's happened to that damned Ricky?

Dottie Oh, he—went out.

Don He'd better stay out. You having him here and kidding me he was someone else.

Dottie That was only to spare your feelings.

Don Thank you; I'll spare his feelings ...

Dottie He *is* Fred's s ... oh, by the way, Fred's coming home tomorrow.

Don Is he though? Good job it isn't tonight. Come on, let's go upstairs.

Dottie After this? Of course not. With Leila knowing.

Don That makes no difference. She'll divorce me anyhow; you know that, don't you?

Dottie Oh, nonsense.

Don She's been wanting to. She's told me so. And now here's her chance, cut and dried.

Dottie But you don't want that.

Don Me? No, of course I don't.

Dottie You still love Leila.

Don Well—I would if she'd let me.

Dottie And you're married. Marriage ought to mean something above all that.

Don I daresay it should. But if you go and break it up—confessing to her with your usual brilliance.

Dottie Don, don't be rude and angry like that.

Don What do you expect? Both my marriages gone west. The first one thanks to your bloody Ricky and now this.

Dottie Ricky only did what you've been doing.

Don Not at all. Mabel was married to me. You're married to an incapacitated old crock who can't function.

Dottie Don't speak like that of Fred. He loves me even if he can't still manage. (*With a sudden thought*) And whatever happens—listen to me; listen to me. Fred must never never be told. If he got to find out about me with you he'd have another stroke and die.

Don Oh, rubbish. Fred's not senile. He's only just seventy.

Dottie Seventy is senile with getting strokes.

Don And don't kid yourself he won't find out. If Leila brings a divorce she'll cite you as co-respondent.

Dottie Rubbish. Leila would never do that. I'll speak to her myself and tell her not to. I can make her understand that you don't really mean a thing to me ...

Don Oh, indeed?

Dottie Or me to you. It's simply been relief for both of us. It didn't count for anything else.

Don Is that all I've meant to you?

Dottie Yes, and me to you. You know that as well as I do.

Don Well, you began it.

Dottie Oh, Don, that's not true. You persuaded me.

Don You didn't need much persuasion.

Dottie I did it more for your sake than my own. I'd never have forced myself to give way if you hadn't suggested it.

Don (*relaxing*) Well, never mind all that. Come on, let's have one more go.

Dottie (*firmly*) No, Don.

Don It may be our last chance for a long time.

Dottie It's no good, Don; I say no. It's always the woman that says.

Don (*indignantly*) Well, what am I supposed to be here for?

Dottie I don't want you here. No, I'm sorry, that's unkind. But do please go. Never mind about dinner.

Don Dinner—who wants to go and eat dinner when we might be ...

Pause

Dottie, relaxed, shakes her head with a gentle smile

Dottie No, we mightn't.

Don becomes indignant

Don God, what a bloody mess-up all round. A nice evening's job you've done. You're an imbecile—that's what you are, an imbecile. (*He strides to the front door. He halts and recovers himself*) No, forget it. I'm sorry. Oh, come on, Dottie.

Dottie Darling, you mustn't go to bed with an imbecile. You might get prosecuted.

Don emits an angry muffled exclamation

Don exits through the front door, slamming it behind him

CURTAIN

SCENE 3

The same. Some hours later

The window curtains are drawn and the lights are on

Leila, in an evening dress, is lying full-length on the sofa. She is in a giggly, pleasant stage of intoxication

Ricky is sitting apart. He is quite sober, very tolerant and friendly towards Leila but a bit bored

Leila (*as if calling*) Rik-ky ...
Ricky That's all right; I'm still here.
Leila Why are you sunnly so aloof?
Ricky A what?
Leila Loof. You were so bright all through dinner. You literally sparkled. Oh, come on.
Ricky Come on whither?
Leila Come and sit beside me. I feel like being sat beside.

Ricky rises

Ricky Certainly. Anything to oblige. But there isn't much room, Leila.
Leila There is if I move my legs. (*She moves her legs down with an effort*) There now.

Ricky sits beside Leila

Like in the taxi. You kissed me when we got in the taxi.
Ricky I'm very well-mannered.
Leila You put your arm round me too.
Ricky You requested me to lend support.
Leila You put it here.
Ricky I couldn't avoid that. You put your arm up.
Leila Did I? Like this? (*She giggles and raises her arm*)
Ricky Yes, and then clamped it down on my hand.
Leila Did I? Like this? (*She giggles again*)
Ricky Yes. An even firmer clamp.
Leila Let's do it again. Don't you want to?
Ricky By all means if you wish. It makes a nice change. I was on the other side before.
Leila (*holding her bosoms*) Oh, I think they're both much the same. What's the matter, Ricky? I don't think you're being very forward.
Ricky I was backward as a boy. I've never caught up.
Leila What are we here for anyway?
Ricky I told you. I phoned Dottie and she said bring you here.
Leila Why didn't we go to my house?
Ricky No, thank you. Your husband may be there by now.
Leila Huh! Don's safely upstairs in bed with Dottie.

Dottie enters from the room L carrying a tray on which are two cups of black coffee. She is wearing a chic garment like a sort of dressy peignoir with a zip at the back and slippers

Ricky rises as she enters

Dottie's manner is rather bossy and impatient

Dottie Here you are—black coffee. That may help. (*To Ricky*) How is she?
Ricky Better. But I'm not sure better than what.
Dottie I did so want her to be talkable-to. (*To Leila*) Here, take this and drink it; it'll do you good. Drink it in sips.
Leila All right, I know; I've done it before.
Dottie (*to Ricky*) I'm very glad you telephoned.
Ricky I wanted to steer clear of Don.
Dottie I told you what he said about Leila divorcing him. Absurd of course but I thought I'd better see her again at once. But I wanted to see her sober. You never told me she was drunk on the telephone.
Leila I'm not drunk. What a vulgar expression.
Dottie Then sip that coffee and get sober. I want to talk to you about you and me and Don.
Ricky (*confidentially*) I doubt if she's in the right shape tonight.
Dottie Then I'll have to leave it over till the morning.
Ricky Oh, then she's sleeping here, is she? Where? In your bed? With you?
Dottie No, I'd rather she didn't do that.
Leila That goes for me too.
Dottie Do you mind if she has your bed?
Leila No, I don't mind.
Dottie (*ignoring Leila*) And you sleep down here on the sofa?
Ricky (*with a sigh*) Oh, all right, Dottie. Anything you say.
Leila I like it on sofas too.
Dottie Thank you, Ricky. Would you mind going and putting on your pyjamas?
Ricky Not at all but I haven't got any.
Dottie Well, you can wear Fred's bath-gown. It's in my room.
Ricky Righto. I can do with a cold shower too. (*He glances at Leila*) And I don't think I'm the only one.

Ricky exits upstairs

Dottie moves to Leila, takes the cup from her and puts it on the small table. She sits beside Leila, her manner becoming much more amicable

Dottie There. Now you're more yourself, aren't you?
Leila How can I be more? I'm myself already. (*She laughs*)
Dottie That's right, darling. You're looking better.
Leila I'm only feeling a little bit sort of vague.
Dottie You're not really angry, are you—about me and Don?
Leila Yes, I am; I'm furious.
Dottie It's all over between us, Leila.

Leila Oh, don't say that.

Dottie I mean between me and Don. We never went to bed you know—tonight I mean.

Leila Why did you ever? Did you really like it with Don? He's so bossy.

Dottie Poor Don, he was wanting. Well, I was too.

Leila He's never had much sense of humour about it, has he?

Dottie No, but I didn't bother about that. I was always in too much of a hurry.

Leila I'd like it with *Ricky*. He's got some fun. But he doesn't seem eager.

Dottie (*gently*) Men don't get very eager about girls who are feeling vague.

Leila You'd like it with him too, wouldn't you?

Dottie (*self-consciously*) I? Oh, but Leila, I couldn't.

Leila Why what's stopping you?

Dottie Ricky's my step-son. It's one of the things you're not supposed to do.

Leila Who says so?

Dottie I think it's in the prayer-book—a woman may not marry—oh, that's marriage. But I expect the prayer-book means going to bed with too. You never quite know—they're always altering the prayer-book. (*Becoming more persuasive and pressing*) But never mind that now. Listen, Leila dear. Finding Ricky here will upset Fred very badly to begin with. Then—this is the real point, darling. If, on top of that, Fred gets to know about Don and me it will kill him. And you don't want that—you like old Fred.

Leila Of course I do. I love him. At times.

Dottie Yes, like you do me. And you don't really want to divorce Don, do you?

Leila I most certainly do. He asked for it.

Dottie That only gives you the opportunity to be kind. Go on, forgive him and take him back.

Leila I don't mind forgiving him but I'm damned if I shall take him back.

Dottie Oh, do, Leila. He'd love you to. And I'm through with him you know. So don't be afraid of hurting my feelings.

Ricky enters from upstairs. He is wearing Fred's bath-gown and an old pair of slippers

Ricky (*as he enters*) All clear.

Leila Oh, look at him. He's all undressed.

Ricky Sorry, not quite all.

Ricky indicates to Dottie to get rid of Leila. Dottie responds readily

Dottie Yes. So come along, Leila. (*Authoritatively*) First on the left up-stairs.

Dottie helps Leila up off the sofa

You won't want a nightie this weather.

Leila Who said I wanted a nightie?

Dottie Pop along now. You don't need any help.

Leila I don't seem to be getting it anyway.

Dottie Get into bed by yourself. Anybody can do that.

Leila Yes, but not many people have to.

Leila exits upstairs unsteadily

Dottie turns to Ricky

Ricky Thanks for the dinner Dottie. I've got the change upstairs. There isn't much of it.

Dottie That's all right. I'm sorry to have landed you with her. I had to get rid of her to get rid of Don.

Ricky (*waving this aside*) I know. That's okay. We're alone again. That's what I've been waiting for.

Dottie Oh, Ricky—me too.

Ricky holds Dottie and kisses her. After a few moments Dottie pulls away, then takes Ricky and kisses him

Dottie I shouldn't have done that, should I?

Ricky Done what?

Dottie Kissed you back like that. I've been feeling like it ever since you went to Harrods.

Ricky It happens that way. You only have to meet someone for five minutes.

Dottie Yes, but isn't it awful our being the someones?

Ricky What's awful about it?

Dottie Darling, don't you see? Whether Fred lets you stay or not, there won't be anything we can do about it.

Ricky That's tomorrow. We don't have to think of that now.

Dottie Oh, but yes, we do ...

Ricky Oh, but no, we don't. I'll get bunged out all right, especially now with Don on the war-path. We may not see each other again for years.

Dottie That's what I mean. It would be so awful to have begun and not be able to go on.

Ricky Dottie, we can't begin considering things the way we are.

Dottie I don't want to consider; I'm simply bursting not to. I'm only saying we couldn't go on being sorry that we weren't still having a lovely time together if we'd never had one.

Ricky We'd be sorrier still never to have had it.

Dottie But think how we might yearn to go on. I don't want to have to yearn. It only drives me to do silly sorts of Don things. (*Refectively, as if to herself*) Of course most people would say "if it's the only chance you'll get why not take it?"

Ricky (*laughing*) That's the best consideration of all.

Ricky kisses Dottie

Have you got anything on under this thing?

Dottie Darling, in this heat? What do you suppose.

Ricky Wouldn't we get on better without it?

Dottie Oh, Ricky—down here?

Ricky Leila says she likes it on sofas. I should think she's a pretty good expert.

Dottie She might come down again.
Ricky Not likely. It was all she could do to get up.
Dottie I wish I didn't feel this little sort of forbidding thing about it. (*Pause*) It unzips at the back of the neck; I don't know why.
Ricky I do. They make them that way so that the gentleman can assist the lady. (*Ricky moves to unzip Dottie's dress*)

Dottie stops him

Dottie No, wait a moment. I know now what that little thought is.
Ricky Oh, Dottie, don't have thoughts.
Dottie No, listen. With Don it was just relief-giving. Just one of those things you have to have, like food and hair-do's. With me there was no more moral harm in it than having a good meal. You see people come into restaurants . . .
Ricky Dottie, we can't have people in restaurants now.
Dottie No, you must let me tell you. They sit at the table, all smiles and gloating over the menu and their stomachs ooze nearer and nearer the table in anticipation; and they get the meal and although it may not be nearly as good as it looked on the menu, it gives them satisfaction and they go away and forget it. Going with Don didn't mean any more to me than that—just a sort of meal. It simply didn't count between me and Fred. With you—oh, Ricky, I think you'd count.
Ricky You mean you honestly feel like that about me? Already?
Dottie (*vehemently*) Good God, you needn't think I want to. I can't help it. With you it would make me feel guilty towards Fred.
Ricky Well, I'd hate to saddle you with a guilty conscience. But when it's something you can't resist—like this.

Ricky kisses Dottie

Oh, Dottie, can't you square your conscience—when you simply can't help it . . .?
Dottie I don't want to have to. I've never had a guilty conscience—I don't want to begin one—(*She puts her hand to the back of her neck*) You have to undo a little catch thing at the top.

Ricky unzips Dottie's dress. It begins to slide off her shoulders

The door bell rings. Ricky steps back. Dottie holds up her dress

Don (*off, in a mild tone*) Dottie . . .

Ricky has an outburst of anger but keeps his voice low

Ricky Oh, damn and blast that man.
Dottie 'Sh, Ricky . . .
Ricky Why should I hush? I hated him before and now I bloody well detest him.
Don (*off*) Dottie—open up. Do please.
Dottie It may be meant.
Ricky What do you mean—meant?

Dottie By providence. To stop us when we shouldn't.

Ricky Don Raeburn is hardly my idea of providence.

Don (*off*) Dottie, I know you're there—lights on and everything. Please, Dottie ...

Dottie I *must* let him in. We'll have trouble with the neighbours. Zip me up, darling. (*She calls*) All right—one minute.

Ricky zips up Dottie's dress, controlling himself

Ricky Sorry. But, damn it, I'm only human.

Dottie Go up to my room. I'll get rid of him.

Ricky Send him home. He'll have a nice big bed all to himself.

Ricky exits upstairs

Dottie goes to open the front door

Don enters. At the outset his manner is penitent and pacific. He moves downstage

Dottie closes the door and follows Don

Dottie Don, what on earth have you come back for?

Don I had to see you again. Leaving you like that—I'm so deeply sorry.

Dottie Oh, is that all it is?

Don Please forgive me. I behaved almost like a cad. I lost control of myself. I was so—terse.

Dottie Never mind. I forgive you. Of course I do. (*She kisses Don abruptly on the cheek*) There.

Don Thank you. That's my kind darling. Oh, I wish I'd stayed with you.

Dottie What for? You're not going to begin that again, are you?

Don I suppose I've left it a bit late. That stinking Ricky's back here now. I heard his voice through the door.

Dottie We were just going to bed. I mean to each other's. To our—each ones.

Don It was really finding him here made me so terse.

Dottie Don't start on him again either. Now run along.

Don Well, give us a little kiss.

Dottie No. No more kisses of any size. Do you want to make things worse with Leila?

Don Leila, yes—she's not come home. Where is she?

Dottie I'm seeing to Leila. She came back here. She's upstairs in my spare bedroom.

Don Thank God she's somewhere. Here—wait a minute. You told me Ricky was sleeping there.

Dottie He's sleeping on this sofa.

Don (*tersely*) Then where is he now? I'm not having Leila stay in the house with that feller. Have they met?

Dottie (*irritated*) Don't be a fool; of course they've met. They met when Leila first came.

Don While I was outside that back door?

Dottie Yes. I only wish you were there now.

Don And both went out. (*With sudden suspicion*) You're not telling me they went out to dinner together?

Dottie Well, I had to get Leila out of the way, didn't I?

Don You sent her out with that skunk?

Dottie Oh, shut up about him and go home.

Don That bastard, taking over each of my wives in turn.

Dottie Only for dinner. You don't suppose he raped her on a table at the Café Royal, do you?

Don I know his way with women. And you've got 'em both back here— together, upstairs there now.

Ricky enters quickly from upstairs

Ricky You leave Dottie alone.

Don Oh, no. Stripped for action already. You don't waste much time.

Ricky Only when talking to you.

Dottie (*to Don*) Stop being idiotic. If you can get Leila to go home with you take her.

Don (*after a moment's hesitation*) My God, I'll settle this.

Don exits hurriedly upstairs

Dottie Did you ever know such a muddle-headed pest?

Ricky No, but I won't have you lugged into it.

Dottie I'm not. I always lug myself.

Don and Leila are heard quarrelling indignantly

Leila (*off*) What d'you think you're doing here? Get out.

Don (*off*) You can't behave like this. Just look at you. Get dressed at once and come home with me.

Leila (*off*) I'm not on stinking terms with you, you speaker.

Ricky I guess it's understandable. He has a precedent.

Dottie Oh, for heaven's sake don't encourage him.

Don enters angrily from upstairs

Don I knew it—she's been got at. Sitting there on his bed stark naked.

Dottie Yes. Waiting to get into bed ...

Don And half soused. That's his game—get 'em soused. I remember that.

Ricky (*trying to quieten Dottie*) Never mind him, Dottie.

Dottie (*ignoring Ricky*) Ricky phoned and I said yes, bring her back here.

Don Just as I said ...

Dottie It was I who wanted her back ...

Don Then why is she waiting naked on his bed?

Dottie (*emphatically*) Because she said she wanted to be put up.

Leila comes to the foot of the stairs. She is naked but holding her dress over part of herself

Leila Who let him in? Coming here disturbing the place—peace ...

Dottie Go back, Leila. You'll catch cold.

Leila Cold? I'm bloody well boiling.
Don That'll do, Leila. Get dressed and come home.
Leila With you? Not likely. Go home yourself and sleep with the cat.
Dottie (*to Don*) Yes, go, will you? She's perfectly safe here.
Leila Go on, d'you hear? Get out.
Don I will. I've seen all I want.
Leila That's just as well. It's the last look you'll ever get.

Leila exits upstairs

Don turns on Dottie

Don After all I've done for you—letting me down like this ...
Ricky Leave her alone, will you? (*He moves to assault Don*)

Dottie stops him

Dottie No, Ricky; you'll only make it worse.
Don Worse for *him* all right. First Mabel and now he's after Leila.

Don moves upstage to the front door and pauses

Fred's going to have the time of his life tomorrow.

Don opens the door. Dottie hurries to him, closes the door and brings Don downstage

Dottie Wait, Don—come here—listen. Ricky didn't even attempt Leila. He refused to.
Ricky Oh, let him do his damn worst.
Don Refused? Huh. He'd do any woman that comes along. You don't know what he's like.
Dottie I do know what he's like.
Don Not only that, he's a bloody crook.
Dottie He's not. He *said* he wasn't.
Don I'll bet he did. To get you to take him in.
Dottie I took him in because I wanted him here.
Don Wanted him?
Dottie (*losing control*) Yes, wanted him.
Ricky Stop it, Dottie.
Don Wanted him in what way? (*Changing tone*) Oh, so that's it, is it?
Dottie What's it?
Ricky No, Dottie ...
Don Getting him here and giving me the go-by. I thought you seemed a bit odd.
Dottie I was not odd. I'm never odd.
Don So you've fallen for this bastard too?
Ricky Don't go on, Dottie. He's not worth it.
Don My God, if this is what I think ...
Ricky What you think you'll find in the sewage ...
Don Wanted him, did you? And fobbed me off to get him.
Dottie You muddling fool, you've just accused him of Leila.

Don Oh, no doubt he tried her too. Thank God she took his measure, even when soused. So then it was *your* turn.

Ricky tries to get at Don. Dottie prevents him

Dottie No, Ricky . . .
Don You can't fool me. Come on, own up.
Dottie Own what up? And why should I?
Ricky Stop baiting her, will you.
Don (*to Dottie*) Come on—let's have it—admit it.
Dottie I won't. As if I would. As if I'd tell anybody, even if it wasn't true.
Ricky (*correcting her*) Was.
Dottie (*indignantly to Ricky*) Was what?
Ricky You mean if it *was* true.
Dottie I'm saying it *wasn't*, aren't I?
Ricky I wouldn't say anything.
Dottie I'm not saying it; he is.
Don Yes, I am. After all I've been to you. Turning me out of your bed and putting him in.
Dottie (*wildly*) Well, who wouldn't.
Ricky Oh, my God.
Don Know what he's like, do you? He's the lowest rotten character I've ever met.
Dottie He's not. Even if he was. Women don't go to bed with men's characters.
Don All that sentimental tripe—"Fred mustn't know about us; it would kill him." My God, when Fred gets to know about *this* . . . (*He moves towards the hall*)
Dottie What do you mean? Are you out of your mind? (*She looks despairingly at Ricky*)

Ricky makes a reassuring gesture

Don calls upstairs

Don Leila, get dressed and come home. (*Pause*) Leila . . .
Leila (*off*) I . . . AM . . . ASLEEP!

Don opens the front door

Ricky (*shouting at Don*) If you say a word against Dottie I'll kill you.
Don I don't have to. It isn't Dottie, it's you. This is the end of you. You wait till I see Fred.

Don exits, shutting the front door behind him

Dottie calls loudly

Dottie No, Don—Don—Don . . .
Leila (*off*) Oh, shut up.

Dottie returns slowly to the living-room

Dottie (*gently*) Impetuous goop. Oh, and I was impetuous too, wasn't I?

Ricky (*kindly*) Well, Dottie, you were a tiny bit admissive.

Dottie He goaded me into it.

Ricky Don't worry. He daren't say a word about you to the old man.

Dottie He'd better try. But it's you. I may have gone and ruined your chances with Fred. Oh, darling Ricky, I'm so sorry.

Dottie embraces Ricky and they kiss

And now it means never for us, never. Forgive me, Ricky.

Ricky Forgive *you*? I'd forgive you anything you do or have done or ever will do.

Dottie and Rickie part. Dottie moves upstage

Dottie It's all my fault.

Ricky Nothing's ever your fault.

Dottie It is. Everything always is. I'm such a fool. Oh, why am I such a fool.

Ricky Because if you weren't you wouldn't be half such a darling.

Dottie (*half laughing, half crying*) I wouldn't. Would I?

Dottie turns and goes slowly upstairs

Ricky watches her go

CURTAIN

ACT II

Scene 1

The same. Next morning, shortly before ten o'clock

When the Curtain *rises Dottie, wearing a pretty dress and a bright apron, is smoothing the sofa. She rearranges the cushions with great care, steps back and surveys the result*

> *Dottie moves into the hall and exits off* L, *speaking as she disappears*

Dottie Don't wash the breakfast things, Ricky. Leave them in the sink.

Leila enters from upstairs, dressed in her overnight dress. She is feeling the effects of the night before and is not in a very agreeable mood

Leila moves to the telephone and brings it to the sofa. A cushion is in her way and she throws it to the ground as she sits down. She dials and listens

> *Dottie enters from* L *of the hall and seeing the cushion on the floor speaks protestingly*

Oh, Leila!

Dottie picks up the cushion and tries to replace it but Leila is in her way and makes no effort to help

Who are you ringing up?

Leila I'm seeing if Don's left for the City. I'm not going home while he's there.

Dottie But you want to see him and tell him what you told me upstairs— that you'll agree to be separated and not divorced.

Leila I didn't say that. I think he's gone. He doesn't answer.

Dottie Perhaps he's still in his bath. But, Leila, you did say that. Though I don't know why you even want to be separated.

Leila Don't keep talking while I'm trying to phone.

Dottie It doesn't matter my talking if there's no reply.

Leila It does if you're talking drivel.

Ricky enters from L *of the hall*

Ricky Leila, your breakfast's ready.

Leila Don't speak to me of breakfast. (*She hands the telephone to Dottie*) Here, you take this. If he answers just ring off.

Ricky Aren't you feeling like anything?

Leila Yes, I'm feeling like my passport photograph.

Ricky Let me do you a soft-boiled egg.

Leila Oh, don't be disgusting.

Dottie Leila, you're being very hangovery and bad tempered.

Leila I'm not; you are. You're very trying in the morning.

Dottie People always are. It's still going brr brr.

Leila Oh, hang the damned thing up.

Dottie replaces the telephone on the table

Dottie Besides, you *must* see Don. To stop him repeating all that rubbish about last night.

Ricky He won't do that.

Dottie (*to Ricky*) He will about *you*. I've got to break it to Fred that you're here at all. Apart from all this going to bed with people.

Leila Don't you tell Fred about me and Don. That we're parting.

Dottie No, he'd begin arguing whose fault it was. And you're not parting I hope. You'd better go now before Fred gets here.

Leila (*preparing to leave*) All right. (*To Ricky*) I'll do what I can for you with Don.

Ricky Thanks. But I'll probably be out on my ear anyhow.

Dottie (*to Leila*) Ricky can let you know whether he's still here or not.

Leila (*to Ricky*) Yes, you may as well do that. Come and see me at lunch-time. I'll give you a bite of something. (*She goes to the front door*)

Ricky Thank you, I will. That sounds delicious.

Leila opens the front door and promptly closes it again

Leila My God, he's here.

Dottie Fred?

Leila Yes. Someone's helping him out of a car.

Dottie I'll go and do that. Wait in your bedroom, Ricky. Go up quickly.

Ricky Okay. Keep that door shut a minute.

   Ricky exits upstairs

Leila returns to the living-room

   Dottie looks upstairs, then exits through the front door, leaving it ajar

Leila snatches up a newspaper and moves to the table with the roses on. She quickly spreads the newspaper, takes all the roses in a handful from the vase and puts them on the newspaper. She begins replacing the roses in the vase one by one

Dottie (*off*) Goodbye, doctor—thank you so much.

Pause

Fred is heard arriving outside

Fred (*off*) You shouldn't carry that thing. Put it down.

   Dottie enters carrying a suitcase which she puts down in the hall

   Fred enters. He is dressed for the very hot weather. He has a hat and a stick. He tosses the hat aside and puts down the stick

Fred moves downstage ahead of Dottie and sees Leila

   (*Agreeably surprised*) Hallo . . .

Leila turns, moves to Fred and kisses him

Leila Fred, dear—welcome home.
Fred Who let you in, you rascal?
Dottie Leila just popped in for a moment.
Leila I brought you a few roses.
Fred Oh, thank you. But how did you know I was here?
Dottie I told Leila on the phone last night. She won't stay. She knows you're not allowed visitors yet.
Fred Who said I wasn't?
Dottie The sister at the hospital.
Fred Oh, that bitch. But you didn't come to the hospital, my pet.
Dottie The last time I did. Anyhow, Leila knows I want you to myself.
Fred Then why didn't she go before I got here?
Leila How could I when you came before I went?
Dottie Darling, don't let's argue ...
Fred I'm not arguing, my dear girl. I'm simply saying ...
Dottie Come and sit down and rest yourself. Run along, Leila.
Fred Well, come in again soon. (*He sits in the chair*)
Dottie Yes, she will. She said so.
Fred When did she? I didn't hear her.

Leila moves to the front door

Leila Will you finish doing my roses, Dottie?
Dottie Yes, dear. Thank you for them. What a bright idea of yours.
Leila We all get bright ideas at times. Take care of *yours*.

Leila exits, closing the front door behind her

Fred What was that she said—that last bit?
Dottie She said take care of you. As if I wanted telling that. (*She moves near to Fred*) It's lovely to have you back, all contented and restful. Oughtn't you to go to bed?
Fred I've been in bed for nearly a week. I'm sick of the damn thing.
Dottie Well, stay comfy there. I'll take up your suitcase.
Fred Oh Lord—haven't you got a woman yet?
Dottie No, they've got very difficult. It's all been quite manageable—well—until this morning.
Fred Why this morning?
Dottie Well, your coming back so early. I had to get breakfast—for myself of course—and do the washing-up and make the beds.
Fred Beds? Only one bed.
Dottie Yes, I said beds because that's what one says, isn't it? Getting up, getting breakfast, washing up, making the beds.
Fred You say bed-making; you don't say beds-making. (*He chuckles and takes Dottie's hand*) You dear funny thing.

Dottie looks thoughtful and comes to a decision

Dottie Fred darling, I want you to be very loving to me.

Fred Damn it, I always am, aren't I?

Dottie Yes, and you've got to be because I've something to tell you.

Fred (*anxiously*) Dottie—nothing wrong with you?

Dottie No, no. But—somebody's turned up.

Fred Turned up? Who? Where from?

Dottie Sit still. Don't get excited.

Fred I'm not. Who's turned up?

Dottie Ricky.

Pause

Fred glares in front of himself, not looking at Dottie

Fred When?

Dottie Yesterday evening.

Fred Here? To see me?

Dottie Yes.

Fred Where is he now?

Dottie Here.

Fred Here, in this house?

Dottie Yes. I let him stay here. (*Pause*) That's why I said beds by mistake.

Fred It wasn't by mistake. When you said beds you meant beds.

Dottie No, but I knew I had to tell you directly I said beds.

Fred Why didn't you tell me right away before you said beds?

Dottie I was leading up to it.

Fred But you said you said it by mistake.

Dottie Said what?

Fred Beds. (*Pause*) So he's come back into my life, has he?

Dottie Yes and he wants to.

Fred Why? To try and finish me off.

Dottie (*sharply*) I'd encourage him to do that, wouldn't I?

Fred (*more gently*) There, there . . .

Dottie Listen, dear. You ought to make it up with him. You must try to. Please. For my sake.

Fred Why for *your* sake?

Dottie It would make me glad. I'm like that—you know me. But for your sake too. For your own peace of mind. You get these strokes—you can't live for ever . . .

Fred You think I'm suddenly going to pop off, do you?

Dottie Well, there is always that. And think how awful it would be to die hating anybody, especially your own son. I know everybody thinks I'm silly and sentimental but I'm not so damn silly as people think and even if I am they all love me for it and especially you. So Fred darling, do this for me to show me how much you love me.

Pause

Fred glares at Dottie

Fred So he's got round you, has he?

Dottie (*emphatically*) No. (*More quietly*) I just—want to help him.
Fred Go and get him.
Dottie Yes, if you'll be—decent to him.
Fred I'll do what I can for your sake.

Dottie pats Fred's hand

Dottie Thank you. (*She rises, pauses, then turns back to Fred*) You will, won't you?
Fred I've said so.

Dottie goes into the hall and calls upstairs

Dottie Ricky—come down.

Dottie remains upstage

   Ricky comes down the stairs, passes her and enters the living-room

Dottie follows Ricky. Fred will not look at Ricky

Pause

Ricky Hallo, Father.
Fred Where the devil have you been all this time? (*He turns his head to look at Ricky*)
Ricky Australia.
Fred Doing what?
Ricky A lot of things. But without much result.
Fred (*grunting*) Then I was right about that.
Ricky Yes, Father. Like you always are. Right about what?
Fred I said "much good it'll do him".
Ricky Do who? Me? When?
Fred When you stole that money from me.
Dottie (*taken aback*) Stole? (*To Ricky*) Oh, I'm sure you didn't, did you?
Ricky Not exactly.
Dottie (*on edge*) You can't not exactly steal.
Ricky I was guilty gross but not guilty net.
Dottie Oh, don't talk like Income Tax people.
Ricky What happened was—I went to the bank in Nairobi and saw the manager, a chap called Prosser ...
Fred Grant.
Ricky Prosser was the man I saw.
Fred You said the manager. Grant was the manager.
Dottie (*to Ricky*) Do let it be Grant.
Ricky All right; Grant. I'd taken one of Father's cheques and copied his signature on it. I said Father had given it to me to take me to Australia. I told Grant so.
Dottie (*shocked*) Ricky ...
Ricky Then I went home and told Father what I'd done.
Fred Yes and why? You knew I'd find out.
Dottie Oh Fred; he did turn honest about it.

Ricky Father was wonderful. He stopped the cheque and wrote me another.

Dottie Dear Fred. How good and kind.

Fred He forced me into it. I didn't want him disgracing me in gaol.

Dottie Oh, but that showed you were fond of him at heart.

Fred God knows I tried to be; in spite of it all.

Dottie Then go on being now; like we said.

Fred holds out his hand to Dottie. Dottie takes it

Fred (*quietly*) You little know what I went through. (*He turns and speaks with an effort to Ricky*) So here you are again, are you?

Ricky Yes, Father. I heard you'd had these strokes.

Fred Only one. This last one was just a tiddler.

Ricky You're looking fairly all right now.

Fred If I'm *all* right how can I be *fairly* all right?

Dottie Now, Fred ...

Fred You get along, my pet, and leave us alone for a bit.

Dottie (*doubtfully*) Well—I'll take your suitcase up.

Ricky I'll do that.

Dottie No, it's quite light.

Dottie moves towards the hall. The telephone rings. Dottie turns quickly to answer it, speaking as she moves

Dottie Oh, why must somebody—it's so inconsiderate—(*she picks up the receiver*) Yes? Who is it? (*She grimaces at Ricky*) Yes, he's back but he can't speak.

Fred Who's that?

Dottie Don Raeburn.

Fred (*affably*) Ah. What's he want?

Dottie Just enquiring. (*On the phone*) I'm afraid you can't come today.

Fred Of course he can come. Why not?

Dottie (*on the phone*) Oh very well. Come this evening if you must.

Fred Here, let me speak to him.

Dottie No, sit down, dear. (*She puts the receiver down quickly*) Besides, he's rung off. (*She moves to pick up the suitcase*) I'll get your bed ready.

Fred I'm not going to bed.

Dottie Not yet. But you must have your afternoon nap.

Dottie picks up the suitcase and walks to the hall, lingering at the foot of the stairs to listen anxiously to Fred and Ricky

Fred Don Raeburn lives close to here now.

Ricky I know. I don't want any part of *him*.

Fred Why not? You should have great respect for him. You went to bed with his wife.

Dottie makes an involuntary move forwards

Dottie No—oh, yes of course, Mabel. I beg your pardon.

Fred Go on—you run upstairs, my love.

Dottie Well, remember your promise. Don't say anything beastly till I come back.

Dottie exits upstairs, taking the suitcase

Ricky She got mixed up with the Mrs Raeburns. I met this second one last night—just for a moment.

Fred Eh? Dottie said she only telephoned.

Ricky laughs briefly

Ricky That's women all over. They meet and talk and next minute they're yapping to each other on the phone.

Fred (*grunting*) That's true enough.

Ricky My word, Father, there's one thing we can agree about.

Fred What d'you mean? What thing?

Ricky Dottie. What a treasure. She's the kindest-hearted woman I've ever met.

Fred You don't think I need telling that.

Ricky No, and I'm glad for you. It's she who's kept you alive and well.

Fred I haven't *been* well.

Ricky No, but for her you might have been dead.

Fred A fat lot you'd have cared.

Ricky Father, you like to please her—do what she wants.

Fred How do you know what she wants?

Ricky I do know. She wants you to throw your arms open to me and say "At last—my son restored to me. The prodigal returned from the pig-geries of Australia."

Fred That's only because she's so damned good-natured to anybody that comes along.

Ricky You ought to have heard her about you—how she loves you—her devotion to you. It's past belief.

Fred What's that got to do with you?

Ricky I'm grateful for her kindness to me. I think she's an angel. If anybody tried to say a word against her . . .

Fred (*challenging*) Against Dottie? Who's going to?

Ricky No, I was just using an expression.

Fred Then it's a damn silly expression.

Ricky I'm sorry, Father. I know I'm illiterate. Don't forget my education was cut short. Of course nobody can say a word against Dottie and they'd better not.

Fred How could they "better not", if they can't?

Ricky Can't, that's all. I didn't mean better not.

Fred There you are—saying what you don't mean and trying to start an argument. You always did that.

Ricky There's nothing to argue about.

Fred Then why do it.

Ricky I'm not. And why not? Because Dottie said don't.

Fred No, she didn't.

Ricky She did. She told you to be gentle and loving and generous.

Fred Generous—I was waiting for that. I know what you're really after.

Ricky I meant generous in spirit.

Fred Spirit, my arse. You've come here looking for cash. Like you always did.

Ricky I came to see you. But if by-and-by I can—hear from you too—(*adding hastily*)—as Dottie hopes I may . . .

Fred (*irate*) What? You've been trying to get round her about money . . .?

Ricky She began it. Knowing Dottie, you don't have to be told that. She wanted it.

Fred Wanted? She wanted you to come begging to me . . .?

Ricky Of course she did. What a question coming from you—the great Dottie expert.

Fred My money—which is all hers as well . . .

Ricky Would that have ever crossed her mind? No, you reply.

Fred I do not. Just the same as ever. You've always been a blight on my existence—just a bloody scourge. I expect all these years you've really been in quod, haven't you?

Ricky Never. In fact, at one time, I was in the Australian police.

Fred Oh, is that how you dodged it?

Dottie enters hastily from upstairs

Dottie (*severely*) Fred, will you stop being like that. (*Gently*) You promised me you wouldn't darling.

Fred How can I help it with him?

Dottie Remember he's your son. Or do you still believe he isn't?

Fred Who told you about that?

Ricky I told her. It may be true; how should I know. But why take it out on me?

Dottie It isn't Ricky's fault. (*Vehemently*) I only want happiness. Happiness for everybody.

Fred I know you do my love. (*Relaxing*) That's because it's you. (*To Ricky*) All right then—stay here for a bit and we'll talk things over.

Dottie Quietly.

Fred (*loudly*) Well, of course quietly.

Dottie Very well. Now I must see to your meals. You have to have slops.

Fred (*indignantly*) Slops?

Dottie The doctor said so.

Fred That doctor is the biggest slop of the lot. I'll teach him to shake his bloody thermometer at me. I'd like some beef. Fillet.

Dottie That can be for tonight. But just a light lunch. Scrambled egg or something.

Fred (*resignedly*) Oh, all right. (*He points to Ricky*) I bet he'll want more than scrambled egg.

Ricky I'm sorry, I won't be here to lunch, Father, I've got a date.

Fred What? Who with?

UNIVERSITY OF WINNIPEG
LIBRARY
515 Portage Avenue
Winnipeg,
DISCARDED

Ricky looks at Dottie, who agrees readily

Dottie With a man he met on the boat, he told me.
Fred Oh. Cruised home, did you?
Ricky It's the cheapest way.
Fred Who is this man? What's his name?
Ricky Rogers. Bertram Rogers.
Fred Well, give him the go-by. No sooner you get here after all this time than you tool off to lunch with this Rogers.
Dottie How was Ricky to know you'd be so glad to see him?
Fred I suppose there is that about it. (*Amiably, to Ricky*) Come on, then. Are you really sorry for all you did to me?
Ricky I am. And I'll try to prove it to you, Father.
Fred I will say you don't look as bad as you used to. Tell me about yourself. Have you got married?
Ricky No, not once.
Fred Why not? Australian girls are very good lookers.
Ricky Smashing. But they don't go for you much if you're broke.
Fred (*riled*) Didn't I say ...
Dottie (*cutting in*) No, Fred. You were beginning to be nice. Go on being.
Fred Why not if I'm starting to like him? I'm not vindictive. She'll tell you. I'm a genial old bugger, aren't I, dear?
Dottie Oh yes, Fred. Not that you're really old.
Fred All right then. (*To Ricky*) Let it be like you said—the prodigal returned. It calls for something. Can you find the way to the cellar?
Ricky Always.
Dottie You're not supposed to drink, you know.
Fred That's what *they* say.
Dottie But I've got to look after you. (*To Ricky*) The cellar's down a trapdoor thing in the kitchen.
Fred You'll find some bottles there.
Ricky Yes. How many?
Fred Oh, one or two to start with.

Ricky begins to move

Hi—wait a minute.
Ricky Don't change your mind, Father.
Fred Make it the Bollinger.
Ricky Agreed.

Ricky exits L of the hall

Dottie Thank you, dear Fred.
Fred I think he's improved. I suspect you had something to do with that.
Dottie I?
Fred Yes. Maybe you've done him a bit of good already.
Dottie No, I just liked him and wanted to be friendly with him—to him.
Fred Yes and he took full advantage of it.
Dottie Oh no.

Fred Yes, he did. He told me so himself.

Dottie Took advantage?

Fred Of your loving-kindness. He got you to come and plead for him.

Dottie He didn't. That was all me. I told him to let me.

Fred And I'm glad you did, my pet.

Dottie Oh, so am I.

Fred Because you're right. I'm getting on and it's time I forgave him. Don't you fret; I'll keep the peace. So long as nothing happens to upset it.

Dottie Nothing will. (*She looks at the telephone and says determinedly*) I'll soon stop it if it does.

Fred If nothing happens you can't stop it, can you?

Dottie Can't I? I will. You see if I don't.

Fred Don't start talking nonsense. Saying you'll stop something that doesn't begin happening.

Dottie No, because I shall stop it before it does.

Fred But if a thing doesn't begin ...

Dottie No, because everything's so happy and settled now. You're quite right, darling.

Fred Of course I'm right. That'll teach you to argue, won't it?

Dottie Oh, Fred; you know I never argue with you.

Fred Then don't do it, my pet.

Dottie I haven't been. I've just stopped.

Fred Right. Good. But if you've stopped you must have begun, mustn't you?

Dottie One thing's certain. You and Ricky are happy again and you're going to stay that way. (*She kisses Fred*) There. Aren't you?

Fred (*fondly*) Yes, yes, yes, yes.

Dottie (*turning upstage, she calls*) Ricky, hurry up with that bottle. Do you want any more help?

CURTAIN

SCENE 2

The same. Early afternoon

The front-door bell rings

   Dottie enters quickly from L of the hall. She opens the front door

   Don enters, dressed in a dark seersucker City suit

Dottie takes his arm and closes the door quietly, then ushers Don into the living-room

Dottie Fred's asleep upstairs. He went to bed directly after lunch. In fact he fell asleep with his cheese. Why did you phone this morning?

Don (*amiably*) To welcome Fred home. Why wouldn't you let me speak to him?

Dottie Isn't that obvious? You haven't been home, have you?

Don No, I'll see Leila later. I don't want a bust-up with her. I'm very fond of her really.

Dottie I'm so glad. We're all fond of each other really, aren't we?

Don Yes, but come on, Dottie. What do you want me for?

Dottie About last night of course. You were so utterly mistaken and stupid.

Don It was all that blasted Ricky. Has Fred seen him yet?

Dottie Oh yes. And they've made it up.

Don Huh, have they. You wait a bit.

Dottie No, Don. You're not to utter a word of that rubbish about Ricky and me.

Don Don't worry. I can eliminate Mr Ricky without that. He's an absolute skunk, Dottie, and a stoat to boot.

Dottie He's not a skunk. And stoats are dear little animals.

Don No woman's safe with him. I'm sure he was getting at Leila last night; never mind you.

Dottie (*gently*) Oh Don, what can I do to make you less spiteful? Now that you're in such a better mood with me?

Dottie takes Don's arm

Don What? (*Pause*) Hold on—where's that Ricky now?

Dottie Lunching with a friend. Let's sit on the sofa.

Dottie propels Don towards the sofa

Don Yes, all right. (*He halts*) I say—you're not getting at anything, are you?

Dottie lets go of his arm and seats herself on the sofa

Dottie No, no; that's got to be a thing of the past. But it's nice to sort of reminisce. Isn't it?

Dottie pats the sofa beside her. Don sits

Don My God, yes. Let's have a kiss. One of our good old kisses.

Dottie Oh Don, isn't that going rather far. Oh, well—just for the last time.

Dottie and Don kiss on the mouth, then Dottie draws back a few inches

It doesn't mean that I promise anything, Don.

Don Don't pull away like that.

Dottie I can't talk with my tongue in your mouth.

Don Then don't talk.

Dottie No, listen. I don't promise anything but you do. First of all you don't say a word about Ricky and me. Promise that, won't you?

Dottie and Don kiss again. Dottie moves his head up and down with hers, then pulls apart

Then—you'll never say the slightest word to enlighten Fred about you and me.

*Dottie and Don kiss, this time with their heads shaking from side to side.
Again Dottie pulls apart*

Finally—you promise not to say a word to Fred against Ricky?

Don No, I'm damned if I promise that.

Dottie Oh, Don . . .

Don I don't trust him an inch. I *know* he was having a crack at Leila. Where's he gone now?

Dottie I told you. He's lunching with a man he met on the boat called Rogers.

Don Not Bertram Rogers by any chance . . .?

Dottie Oh—I . . .

Don He's with Leila now, isn't he?

Dottie What if he is? That only goes to prove they're just friends.

Don The hell it does.

Dottie Of course it does. I mean—nights, yes. Afternoons, yes—well, you know that. But at lunch-time . . .

Don This settles it. I'll have his guts.

Dottie No, I tell you. It'll upset Fred. Just when I've got him so happy and placid.

Fred comes downstairs, disgruntled

Dottie and Don hear him coming

Fred (*off*) Dottie . . .

Fred enters the living-room, wearing his bath-robe

Dottie Fred—you shouldn't be up.

Fred I'm not up, I'm down. Hallo, Don.

Don Fred—I'm glad to see you.

Dottie Why aren't you still asleep?

Fred Because I'm awake. I want a hot-water bottle.

Dottie Hot-water . . . but it's a heat-wave. Didn't you know that?

Fred I don't care—my feet get cold. (*To Don*) You've got here good and early.

Don I wanted to talk to you. But Dottie said you were asleep.

Dottie So he will be when he gets his bottle.

Don Then go and get it, my pet.

Dottie Only if you go straight back to bed.

Fred What's the use if I don't have the bottle.

Dottie You'll have it directly it's ready.

Fred And meanwhile my feet will get colder still.

Dottie That's why I'm going to bring you the bottle.

Fred Oh, why must you always argue? Have it your own way; you always do. Come on, Don, you can talk to me upstairs.

Dottie No, certainly not. You'll keep him awake.

Don Wake him up more likely.

Dottie Very well, *I'll* tell him. He's trying to make you get rid of Ricky again.

Fred Why, what's he been up to now?

Dottie He hasn't. It's simply revenge on Don's part. Revenge is a terrible thing, so brutal and unrefined. Besides, it's an absolute lie.

Fred What is for heaven's sake?

Leila and Ricky enter together through the front door

Dottie Here's Ricky now; he'll tell you himself.

Don You see—the two of them.

Leila Hallo, Fred. (*She sees Don and speaks challengingly*) What are you doing here?

Don What are you? With him.

Leila I came to see Fred.

Don When you thought he was in bed asleep.

Leila Well, why isn't he?

Dottie He's got cold feet.

Leila Then get him a hot-water bottle.

Dottie Don't you begin that.

Ricky (*indicating Don*) I know why he's here. Go on, tell the old man. We all know you're a damned liar.

Fred What is all this?

Leila I'll tell you. To begin with Don and I are parting.

Don I don't say that.

Leila Then I do.

Fred But why? What the hell's happened?

Dottie Don's been having a silly little affair with someone and now he says someone else has been after Leila.

Fred (*sharply*) What? Who has?

Dottie It's only a squabble. It's nothing to do with you, dear.

Don Oh, isn't it?

Fred (*angrily to Don*) You say it *is*? With *me*? What the devil are you insinuating? About me?

Leila And me? (*Sarcastically to Fred*) Oh, too bad, darling, we've been found out.

Fred My God, do you dare ...?

Dottie No, Fred, he doesn't. How could he?

Don Don't be absurd. An old friend of your integrity.

Ricky Take it easy, Father. He knows you couldn't.

Fred No, he doesn't.

Dottie Of course he must. Don't be silly, Fred. At your age and with strokes and things.

Leila (*sarcastically*) Willing as little Leila was no doubt.

Fred Then what the ...?

Dottie Be quiet. Keep calm and sit down.

Dottie attends to Fred, who calms down

There. Now, listen. I put Leila up last night in the spare-room ...

Fred Why?

Dottie She didn't want to be with Don.

Fred Why not?

Dottie Because they think they've parted. You've been told that. Do listen to what people say. Don says Ricky wanted to go to bed with Leila.

Fred And did he?

Ricky I wasn't even trying to. (*To Leila*) Was I?

Leila No, and I had some option in the matter, didn't I? (*Angrily to Don*) My God, this is pretty rich, coming from you.

Don I know you wouldn't let him but I know him of old.

Dottie Yes, but Leila's not like Mabel. (*To Ricky*) Is she?

Ricky (*indicating Don*) I'm afraid he's the only one who knows that.

Fred begins to chuckle

Fred Ho ho ho—poor old Don. (*His chuckle grows into a laugh*)

Don What's funny about it I'd like to know. (*To Dottie*) Is this another stroke?

Dottie (*anxiously*) No, he doesn't laugh when he strikes. Fred, dear . . .

Fred Sorry—it's just the idea—each of your wives in turn. Same chap. Second innings. I can't help it—I think it's damn funny.

Don Well, I don't. I've all the more reason for suspecting.

Leila Suspecting me?

Don Yes. No. Him anyhow. He's still at it. He went to lunch with you.

Fred He did not. He lunched with a feller called Rogers. Didn't you?

Ricky I changed my mind, Father.

Fred (*testily*) You went out saying you were meeting Rogers.

Ricky (*also testily*) I can have changed my mind outside, can't I?

Fred Then why go to her instead of coming back?

Dottie That was for my sake. I told him I was glad he was going out. There weren't enough eggs.

Don Rubbish. It was all pre-arranged. Dottie herself told me so.

Ricky That's a lie. Dottie wasn't in it. I fixed it with Leila myself.

Fred (*to Don*) And don't you start saying things about Dottie.

Dottie Yes, I did tell him, Ricky.

Leila Oh, stop it. I told Ricky to come and tell me whether he'd been accepted back.

Dottie That was before he knew.

Leila When he did know, you idiot.

Dottie Leila, don't be rude. You've been like that all day.

Fred That'll do now. I want to know. What—is—all—this—about?

Dottie I've told you . . .

Ricky Listen, Father . . .

Fred Shut up.

Dottie It's only Don trying to get at Ricky.

Fred (*glaring at Ricky*) Looks like you've been got at yourself.

Don Yes, to let him take Leila to dinner and back here.

Fred (*loudly*) And shut up you.

Dottie Fred, don't shout. It's bad for you. And all the windows are open.

Fred (*to Ricky*) Is it true what he says? Did you roger Leila last night?

Leila Don't talk as if I were a tart. It takes two, you know. Or have you forgotten?

Fred Whether he did or not that's not the point.

Don Oh, isn't it?

Fred I've told you to shut up, haven't I?

Fred turns on Ricky, igniting another past quarrel

You. All these lies about lunch and some bloody Rogers. And mixing Dottie up in it.

Dottie He didn't. I mixed myself up.

Fred No. I know you better than that. (*To Ricky*) You implicated her.

Ricky In what? What are you accusing Dottie of?

Fred (*furiously*) Accusing her? You dare say that?

Ricky I know what you're like at false accusations.

Fred Don't you answer me back. It's the same old story.

Ricky A pretty dirty story on your part.

Fred The same old lies and intrigues.

Dottie Fred, will you stop.

Fred No, I damn well won't when you've been used this way.

Don He got her to say he was a cousin.

Fred (*rounding on Don*) For the last time—shut your mouth.

Leila Time, gentlemen, please.

Fred You forced yourself on Dottie; cashed in on her good nature ...

Dottie He did not. It was all me. But for me he wouldn't be here.

Ricky I wouldn't want to be. And if Dottie wasn't Dottie she wouldn't.

Fred Are you trying to poison my mind against her?

Ricky Nothing could poison your mind.

Fred So it's Dottie you wanted to stay for?

Ricky Yes, so long as it's without you.

Fred What? Have you been trying to lay hands on her?

Dottie Fred, how dare you say that? I wouldn't let him.

Fred Oh—then he did try to?

Ricky (*pointing to Don*) You're as bad as he is. You can't go lower than that.

Dottie Don't irritate your father, Ricky.

Ricky Why not? With any luck he'll burst.

Fred (*exploding*) That's all from you, you bastard. And when I say bastard I mean it.

Ricky I'm glad of that anyhow.

Fred Whatever you've done before this beats the lot. You're nothing but a lying, sneaking, forging, fornicating pariah. I can't stand this, I'm going to my room. And you can pack your bloody bag and get out of my sight. I never want to set eyes on you again.

Don Well done, Fred.

Fred And damn you too.

Fred exits upstairs

Ricky turns to Dottie

Dottie Fred.
Ricky Father.
Dottie Let him be. He'll simmer down and say he's sorry.
Ricky Not to me. He won't get the chance.
Don No, that he won't.
Dottie Yes, he will. (*To Ricky*) But do what he says. It may soothe him if he hears you pretending to pack.
Ricky (*resignedly*) Oh, what's the use. (*He moves towards the hall*)
Don Not much pretending about it. He heard what Fred said to him.
Ricky You weren't altogether complimented.

Ricky exits upstairs

Leila laughs

Don And what are you giggling about?
Leila I'd just love to hear what Fred would say if he was told about *you* two.
Dottie Oh, will you stop harping on that. I don't matter. You do—to Don I mean. You're his wife. You loved him and married him and enjoyed him. Didn't you?
Leila (*heedlessly*) He was all right up to about half-time.
Dottie But it shouldn't be even half-time with you yet. You're young and Don's still quite vigorous. I loathe the way he's been about Ricky; I think he's been atrocious. But do take him back, Leila. He loves you. He really does.
Leila Loves me from inside your bed.
Dottie Of course. That's why he didn't want you to know where he was. You don't want to part, do you, Don?
Don I never said I did.
Leila I've told him I'm bored with the very sight of him. Especially with nothing on.
Don There's no call to be personal.
Dottie I know what you mean, but you don't have to look at him all the time. Oh, do be reconciled. It will help me so. I won't have to think any more about you.
Don You won't have to think any more about your Ricky, anyhow.
Dottie Yes, I will. I've got to think of Fred too, the state he's in. It's always so hard to know who to have to think of most first.
Leila For goodness sake, Dottie, stop this everlasting saint-upon-earth stuff. It's nauseating.
Dottie (*indignant*) Will you stop being so bitchy when we've always been such friends and still are. All because you drank too much last night.

Ricky's suitcase lands in the hall, thrown there from the top of the stairs

Ricky comes downstairs, glances into the hall and exits off L of the hall

Leila I'm going.
Dottie Yes, do. And, Don, you go with her.

Leila He's going back to his office.

Don No, I'm not. I can go to my own house if I choose, can't I?

Leila I suppose you think you're going to turn me out of it.

Dottie Of course he isn't. You're going to stay there together.

Leila No, thank you. I'll pack some things and go to an hotel. (*She moves upstage*)

Don No, I'll do that.

Dottie Leila, Don, be sensible. You can't both go to hotels. And leave the house empty to be burgled. Besides, think of the poor cat.

Don (*to Leila*) That's all right. You stay in the house. I know where I can go.

Leila You never said a truer word.

Leila exits through the front door, closing it behind her

Dottie Go after her, Don. Be masterful. I know how masterful you can be.

Don Oh, let her stew.

Dottie No, you go and stew her. Go and give her a good smacking and take her to bed.

Don (*moving upstage*) I'll stop her leaving the house, anyhow.

Dottie Yes, do. Before she begins this ridiculous packing.

Don exits through the front door

Ricky enters from L of the hall

Ricky Thank God you've got rid of them.

Dottie Poor Leila; she's being very snooty and uneducated.

Ricky Never mind them—it's us. Oh, Dottie ...

Dottie I'll make it all right with Fred. I can. I promise.

Ricky How can you now? Does he often blow his top like that?

Dottie He gets over it. He will. He must.

Ricky takes Dottie in his arms

Ricky If only it didn't mean parting with you ...

Dottie It's not going to. I'm not going to let it.

Dottie and Ricky embrace, then Dottie disengages herself quickly, looking towards the stairs

Fred comes down the stairs

Fred, what are you doing—creeping down like that?

Fred I heard the front door. I thought it was him going. Why are you still monkeying about with him?

Dottie I was consoling him. After that terrible exhibition of yours.

Fred He was damned insulting to me too.

Ricky Yes, I was. I inherited that.

Dottie Quiet. Both of you. Don't begin it again.

Fred After what he admitted. Hankering after you.

Dottie He didn't admit it. (*To Ricky*) *Did* you? If he did, it wasn't all on Ricky's side.

Fred Oh, yes it was. You said you didn't let him.

Dottie I only didn't because we kept saying we oughtn't to. By the time we'd finished talking about it it was too late anyhow.

Fred (*too dismayed to be angry*) What? But had you no thought for me?

Dottie Yes. That was what we were wasting time talking about.

Fred But, God damn it, you're my wife and he's my son.

Ricky Oh, I am again, am I?

Fred After this? No, never.

Dottie Well, that makes it less complicated. But you're not going to turn him out.

Fred (*angrily*) You think I'm going to let him stay on here?

Dottie He'll be staying tonight, anyhow. (*To Ricky*) Take your bag back to your room.

Fred I won't stand for this.

Ricky Dottie knows best, Father. And there's a lot of that Bollinger left.

Ricky exits upstairs with his suitcase

Fred (*sighing*) It defeats me, Dottie. Ever since he came you've been siding with him against me.

Dottie I've only been trying to keep things happy for everyone. Besides, I'm fond of Ricky. He's your son, all right—he's so endearing.

Fred He's not so damned endearing as I am. You needn't think I haven't twigged—he's after you.

Dottie Even if he was it's only natural.

Fred You egged him on, didn't you?

Dottie Did I? Oh, but, darling; don't forget that at my age I can't help there being times when I feel a bit egged myself.

Fred (*quietly*) Yes, poor girl. I suppose I can't argue about that.

Dottie And Ricky's not like other men in that way.

Fred (*sharply*) What? How do you know he's not?

Dottie Did I say that? I didn't mean to.

Fred What other men? (*Anxiously*) Dottie? You haven't been unfaithful to me?

Dottie No, darling; never. Never. (*After a pause*) Not the way I look at it.

Fred What? . . . Look at what?

Dottie Oh, Fred, there's something I'd like to tell you and have done with it. But perhaps I'd better not.

Fred Come on—what is it?

Dottie I only meant—suppose a man was unhappy at home and wanted someone to be kind to him . . .

Fred This infernal kindness . . .

Dottie I know, I know. I'm feeble about it. I go too far.

Fred But, God almighty, you don't go so far as to let some outsider—do that to you?

Dottie (*hesitating*) Fred—how well are you feeling?

Fred I'm all right. Why? Go on . . .

Dottie Well, listen—do you suppose I'd mind if you'd had some nonsense with a girl—any girl—Leila, for instance?

Fred Eh? Why? You think I've been pulling Leila about?
Dottie You flared up at Don when you thought he said so.
Fred Well, I never dreamed he'd guess. It's simply—I may have fumbled now and then. You know how one does.
Dottie But you'd have gone the whole hog if you could have. And I'd have known it was only poor old nature being rather silly and I'd have forgiven you and gone on loving you the same as ever. Like you would me if it had been the other way round.
Fred Other way round?

Ricky comes down the stairs and stands in the hall

Dottie If instead of it being you with Leila it had been me with Don.
Fred There's no need to make a joke of it.
Dottie But that's just what it all is. I had to keep it from you with your strokes and things. But now, in my heart, oh, darling—it makes me so much happier that you know.

During this speech Fred passes from incredulity to fury

Ricky moves downstage

Fred Don? My God, this is past belief. (*He gets to his feet*)
Dottie Oh, dear; I shouldn't have told you. Hold him down, Ricky.
Ricky Yes, that'll do, Father. Don't overdo it.

Ricky helps Fred back into his chair

Fred (*to Ricky*) Did you know about this?
Ricky No. Well—yes—I—deduced.
Fred Then why didn't you break his bloody neck?
Ricky It's only Dottie's kind nature,
Dottie You said you'd forgive me like I would you.
Fred Of course I forgive you. It's what he says—all this pitying, angelic, God-forsaken kindness. But him—the filthy traitor, oiling in to take advantage of it—Where is he? Ring him up. Get him here.
Dottie Fred—that's no good.
Fred I'll do him no good. (*To Ricky*) Go on. Ring him up.
Ricky I don't know his number.
Fred I'll damn well ring him myself.
Dottie Oh, do sit still. (*She pushes Fred down*) Get him some brandy, Ricky.

Ricky moves to the drinks table

There, darling; don't get too excited.

The door bell rings

Oh, what a time for someone to call. (*To Ricky*) Send whoever it is away. Unless it's the doctor.

Ricky goes into the hall and opens the front door

Don enters. He is animated and delighted. He shouts as he enters

Don Dottie ...
Ricky She says go away.

Don pushes past Ricky and comes downstage

Don Dottie, it's splendid. It's all okay, like you said.

Ricky closes the door and returns to the drinks table

Fred (*to Don, with a menacing growl*) Come here, you.
Don (*heartily*) Oh, hallo, Fred.
Fred Don't you hallo me. This isn't some bloody hunt.

Dottie holds Fred down

Dottie Don't excite him.

Fred tries to free himself from Dottie

Fred Let me be. I want to get at him.
Dottie Then do it sitting down.
Don (*mystified*) What's up now, old boy?

Fred struggles free from Dottie

Fred I'll show you what's up. (*He takes a swing at Don, misses and stumbles back on the sofa*)
Dottie (*to Don*) I've told him about us.
Don (*calmly*) Oh. Why?
Dottie Well, you threatened to yourself. (*To Fred*) Don't get angry darling.
Fred Get? What do you mean "get"?
Don (*airily*) I'm sorry, Fred.
Fred Sorry—I'll make you sorry, you fornicating tick.
Ricky (*taking Fred a glass of brandy*) Try some of this, Father.
Fred You go to hell. (*Changing his mind*) Oh—all right. (*He gulps the brandy in one and hands the glass back to Ricky*)
Dottie You shouldn't gulp it all at once.
Fred You keep your mouth shut. (*Relenting*) No—sorry, my pet.
Don Listen, Fred. I only did it out of kindness to Dottie.
Ricky Oh, my God.
Fred She did it to be kind to *you*, you stinking liar.
Don It was fifty-fifty.
Dottie Yes. Don took pity on me too. Women hanker just as men do. So please forgive him for my sake.
Fred Forgive him? I never want to see his face again. I only wish I could bash it in. Get out of here. (*To Ricky*) Get me some more of that stuff.

Ricky returns to the drinks table

Don speaks confidentially to Dottie

Don Good about me and Leila, isn't it?
Dottie She must have changed her mind very quickly.

Don I caught her up. I had a brainwave. I offered her two thousand quid
to stay with me.
Dottie What a good idea. What did she say?
Don She said five. But only on condition you'll promise never to entertain
me again in that way.
Dottie I've told her that.
Don Yes, but she thinks you may get needful and weaken.
Fred Get off my premises, you shyster.
Don She's still out there. Come and reassure her.
Dottie Well, poor Leila—I don't want her to lose five thousand pounds.

Dottie and Don exit quickly through the front door

*Fred sits in thought for a few moment, then speaks sharply without looking
at Ricky*

Fred Come here, you.
Ricky I *am* here.
Fred Then stay here.
Ricky Oh. Thank you, Father.
Fred Shut up and listen to me.
Ricky Yes—what?
Fred (*looking towards the front door*) Where's Dottie gone?
Ricky She's getting rid of Don. For good.
Fred So I should hope. Poor dear Dottie; having to fall back on a thing
like Don. Why couldn't you have come home sooner? That would have
settled Don's hash.
Ricky Why, how do you mean, Father?
Fred If you'd have been knocking around here all the time she'd have very
soon have given Don the boot.
Ricky I still don't see what you mean?
Fred Don't keep asking me what I mean. You know damn well what I
mean. D'you think I don't see? I know Dottie. I can read her like a
book. You're the one for her. Aren't yer—?

*From now on Ricky listens, incredulous at first, gradually delighted but
restraining himself*

Ricky I—can't help it, Father.
Fred Who the hell wants you to help it?
Ricky (*almost inaudibly*) What?
Fred Here I am—past all that—long past. And Dottie's still young and—
and full of a young woman's—natural impulses and physical thingame-
bobs—desires. (*Challengingly*) Are you telling me that she's got to bottle
herself up and go without? What sort of a fond old husband would I be
if I didn't say to her "You go ahead my pet. You spend you life dishing
out this bloody milk of human kindness to all and sundry. Give yourself
a swig of it when you feel you want it. Give yourself a taste of joy now
and then." Eh? Isn't that her due?
Ricky Yes, Father.

Fred Very well then. If that's how it is, that's how it is. But no more of her having to fall back on some cockeyed Don. Understand?

Ricky (*incredulously*) Yes.

Ricky smiles at Fred but receives no smiling response from the latter who continues seriously

Fred Oh, don't kid yourself. I know where her true lasting happiness lies; it lies with me. But now that's got to be the happiness of affection and contentment. She knows that. As for the other thing—if that *adds* to her happiness and joy of life, well, by God, that's all *I* want. Understand?

Ricky Yes, Father.

Fred Then if you're the one to give it her, the one of her choice, that's up to her. You needn't think you'd be *my* pick but there it is. After all, I suppose it'll be as well to keep it in the family.

Ricky Yes. Thank you, Father.

Fred (*more heatedly*) Don't thank me. I'm not doing it for *you*.

Ricky No, I didn't mean that.

Dottie enters quickly, almost out of breath. She swings the front door to

Dottie It's all fixed; Leila's going to buy herself a new car. (*She comes down, eyeing Fred suspiciously*) Fred—you haven't been quarrelling again.

Fred No, I wouldn't let him. Come here to me, my pet.

Dottie Goodness, I'm hot.

Fred Yes, come and cool down.

Ricky Father has something to tell you.

Fred Keep quiet, you. Leave it to me.

Dottie Leave what? What have you two been talking about?

Fred You. About what you've told me about your feeling like you do sometimes. At your age, when you're so young and now that I'm —(*he pauses*)

Ricky Unable.

Fred (*angrily*) Will you—!

Ricky Sorry. Carry on.

Dottie Darling, sweet Fred. Never mind about that any more. So long as I've got you that's what matters above everything else. Even if I do still get these silly little feelings sometimes.

Fred Yes, and don't think I don't understand about that.

Dottie Darling Fred, you are so loving. You almost make me cry.

Fred No, it stands to reason. Just nature's way. So—listen, my pet. I know how you feel towards this feller—drawn to him or whatever you like to put it. So just to show you how fond I am of you—when you feel it crop up like you say you do—if you want—

Fred pauses, searching to express himself. Dottie half mystified, incredulous as Ricky was

Ricky (*trying to help Fred out*) A lover—

Fred (*indignantly*) Don't you butt in.

Ricky Sorry. I thought you'd dried up. In speech as well, I mean.

Dottie What is all this? What are you saying? (*Harder*) Fred.

Fred I'm only trying to show my love and affection for you.

Dottie Your love and affection? To *tell* me—to be false to you with Ricky? Just to please myself?

Fred (*also harder*) Yes. That's what my love and affection *does* mean.

Dottie What about mine? How can you love me if you think Ricky and I would ... With you knowing?

Fred There you are; you've given yourself away again. By what you've just said.

Dottie I haven't said something, have I?

Fred Yes, you said you'd go with him so long as I didn't know.

Dottie I didn't. And I wouldn't. We could have last night and didn't. I wish we had now—no, I don't mean that. But as for your telling me to—

Ricky Dottie, he *wants* us to. To show his love for you.

Dottie Yes, and I think it's horrifying.

Fred Horrifying? You refuse?

Dottie Of course I do. Oh Fred, I love you so much and always will. Always, always.

Ricky I daresay, but where does that leave me?

Fred Out on your bloody ear, my boy.

Ricky Now wait a minute.

Fred Sorry—I haven't got time. Come on, Dottie—come and put me back to bed.

Dottie Oh, Fred—what would your doctor say?

Dottie and Fred go upstairs together leaving Ricky by himself

Fred (*as he goes*) If you want something to do—fetch another bottle of Bollinger and put it on ice.

CURTAIN

FURNITURE AND PROPERTY LIST

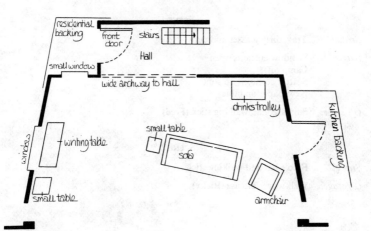

ACT 1

SCENE 1

On stage: Sofa with scatter cushions
Armchair
Small table
Writing table. *On it:* telephone
Table. *On it:* a bowl of roses
Two-tier table. *On it:* decanters, assorted bottles of drink, cut-glass tumblers
Glass with a small amount of whisky and water in it on the floor by the sofa

Personal: **Dottie:** book, shoes on floor by sofa

SCENE 2

Strike: Dirty glasses

Set: Long drink on table beside sofa
Handbag containing a key and some Treasury notes for **Dottie**

Off stage: Well-worn suitcase (**Ricky**)
Bath-gown, small towel (**Don**)

SCENE 3

Strike:	Dirty glasses
Set:	Window curtains closed
Off stage:	Tray holding two cups of black coffee (**Dottie**)

ACT II

SCENE 1

Strike:	Tray, dirty glasses and cups
Set:	Window curtains open Lamp off Scatter cushions on sofa Newspaper on table
Off stage:	Suitcase, hat, walking stick (**Fred**)

SCENE 2

Strike:	Fred's hat and walking stick
Off stage:	Well-worn suitcase (**Ricky**)

LIGHTING PLOT

Property fittings required: pendant light

Interior. A living-room. The same scene throughout

ACT I Scene 1. Afternoon

To open: General interior lighting
No cues

ACT I Scene 2. Late afternoon

To open: General interior lighting
No cues

ACT I Scene 3. Evening

To open: All lamps on
No cues

ACT II Scene 1. Morning

To open: General interior lighting
No cues

ACT II Scene 2. Early afternoon

To open: General interior lighting
No cues

EFFECTS PLOT

ACT I

Cue 1	Shortly after the curtain rises *Door bell rings*	(Page 1)
Cue 2	**Dottie** puts on her other shoe *Door bell rings loudly*	(Page 1)
Cue 3	Shortly after the curtain rises on Scene 2 *Door bell rings*	(Page 8)
Cue 4	**Dottie:** "... I seem to get into" *Door bell rings*	(Page 11)
Cue 5	**Dottie:** "Bring it in here." *Noise of door closing. The telephone rings six or seven times*	(Page 12)
Cue 6	**Dottie:** "No, I've just time ..." *Telephone rings*	(Page 13)
Cue 7	**Don:** "What the hell are you talking about?" *Door bell rings*	(Page 14)
Cue 8	**Don:** "... of finding that bastard here." *Door bell rings*	(Page 14)
Cue 9	**Dottie:** "It can't be helped." *Prolonged ring of door bell*	(Page 15)
Cue 10	As **Dottie's** dress slides of her shoulders *Door bell rings*	(Page 25)

ACT II

Cue 11	**Dottie** moves towards the hall *Telephone rings*	(Page 36)
Cue 12	Shortly after the curtain rises *Door bell rings*	(Page 40)
Cue 13	**Dottie:** "... don't get too excited". *Door bell rings*	(Page 49)